Presented To:

From:

Date:

WISDOM *for* WINNERS

VOLUME TWO

WISDOM for WINNERS

VOLUME TWO

JIM STOVALL

AN OFFICIAL PUBLICATION OF
THE NAPOLEON HILL FOUNDATION

Sound Wisdom

P.O. Box 310

Shippensburg, PA 17257-0310

International rights inquiries please contact The Napoleon Hill Foundation at 276-328-6700

Email: napoleonhill@uvawise.edu

For more information on foreign distributors, call 717-532-3040.

Or reach us on the Internet: www.soundwisdom.com

Cover design by Eileen Rockwell

ISBN 13 HC: 978-0-7684-1038-9
ISBN 13 TP 978-1-937879-49-5
ISBN 13 EBook: 978-0-7684-1039-6

For Worldwide Distribution, Printed in the U.S.A.
1 2 3 4 5 6 / 20 19 18 17 16

CONTENTS

FOREWORD

PERHAPS YOU ARE ONE OF THE MILLIONS OF PEOPLE WHO HAVE enjoyed the 30 books written by Jim Stovall over the years. You may have even watched one of the six movies that were made from Jim Stovall's books. Jim's best-selling book, *The Ultimate Gift*, with over five million copies sold, was one of the books made into a movie. *The Ultimate Gift* book series, along with the movie trilogy, has grossed over $110 million.

When Jim Stovall writes a column on wealth, he does so with authority. A favorite quote of mine from Stovall's *The Millionaire Map*, published by Sound Wisdom, simply states, "Never accept a map from someone who has not been where you want to go." If you would consider that simple statement and the good advice behind it, it could make the difference between you being successful, or just being one of the majority of people who are not.

Jim also wrote a book titled *The Financial Crossroads: The Intersection of Money and Life*, co-authored with Timothy J. Maurer, a certified financial planner. Jim reminds his readers that being motivated is useless if you do not know what to do. Knowing what to do is useless unless you are motivated to act.

Jim Stovall's *Wisdom for Winners* is a collection of columns that millions of people have read over the years. His wisdom and experience on a particular subject provide a great amount of credibility to his writings. Even though Jim has written several columns on overcoming adversity, perhaps for those who do not know his background, a little personal information is worth knowing. Jim aspired to be an NFL player and he had the mental and physical capabilities to be a success. Also, Jim was a heavy-weight Olympic weight lifter, but his plans took a serious challenge.

While attending Oral Roberts University, Jim was diagnosed with macular degeneration, which led to him becoming blind. Tutored by his girlfriend and future wife Crystal, Jim graduated. Most people going blind would just give up and seek government assistance. Not Jim. He told his dad (who was an employee of Oral Roberts University) that he wanted to work for himself. Jim's father introduced Jim to Lee Braxton, a large financial contributor to Oral Roberts University.

Jim was fortunate to be introduced to Braxton, as he was a great example of overcoming adversity and founder of many successful companies, including a bank. Lee Braxton was also a close friend of Napoleon Hill and delivered Hill's eulogy when he died in 1970. Braxton had used the principles found in Napoleon Hill's book *Think and Grow Rich,* and not only learned them, but took action. Braxton introduced Jim Stovall to *Think and Grow Rich,* which helped him become successful in financial and personal matters.

You will certainly be rewarded for reading Jim Stovall's columns on the value of wealth, learning is a lifelong process, mastering your time, doing your best, looking for opportunities, what is important in life, and many other articles found in this volume of Jim Stovall's *Wisdom for Winners*.

While Jim's columns often provide financial advice, his columns also cover important topics such as "What is Important in Life." Jim gives advice on giving that creates a legacy for the giver. Jim tells us that while budgeting our money and making investments can benefit our family, it can also put us in a position to help others.

Jim Stovall writes from his own personal experiences. For example, Jim has provided 500 scholarships for students attending Oral Roberts University. Jim has made many contributions, such as the articles you are about to read. Jim gave his many columns to the nonprofit Napoleon Hill Foundation to raise funds to provide scholarships for the University of Virginia's College at Wise. The Napoleon Hill Foundation also does prison work and has worked to make the success principles available around the world to make the world a better place in which to live.

I hope you enjoy the book, one column of wisdom at a time. Steve Forbes, publisher of *Forbes* magazine, calls Jim, "One of the most outstanding men of this era."

Though a multi-millionaire and one of the most sought-after speakers, Jim can be reached at 5840 South Memorial Drive, Suite 312, Tulsa, OK 74145-9082; by email at Jim@JimStovall.com; on Twitter at www.twitter.com/stovallauthor; or on Facebook at www .facebook.com/jimstovallauthor.

—DON M. GREEN, executive director of the Napoleon Hill Foundation, board member of the University of Virginia/Wise, and president of the University of Virginia/Wise Foundation.

OVERCOMING ADVERSITY

LEARNING AND DOING

RECENTLY, I WAS SPEAKING WITH A PASTOR WHO HAD JUST delivered a rather critical message to his congregation. I was curious whether or not people were offended or took the criticism personally. The pastor laughed and told me the good and the bad news. The good news was that the congregation was not offended because none of them really thought the comments were directed toward them or that they were the focus of his criticism. The bad news was just the same—none of them thought the comments were directed toward them or that they were the focus of his criticism.

Unfortunately, in this life we only learn from mistakes. Most of us only learn from the mistakes we make ourselves. A relatively few more enlightened individuals can observe the world around them and actually learn from the mistakes of others. The sad thing remains that the people who need to learn life's lessons the most are very often the people who listen the least.

This happens because we judge our own intentions and everyone else's actions; therefore, when the boss is already 10 minutes into the meeting where he is describing the importance of punctuality as you slip into the back of the room—embarrassingly late again—you were able to look at your intentions and console yourself with the thoughts that you were not irresponsible and not the kind of person that is normally late. It's just that the toast got burned, the dog got out, the kids were running behind, etc.

On the other hand, when you are feeling self-righteous about being in the meeting on time or even a few minutes early, when one of your colleagues slips in 15 minutes late, in the harsh light of your internal judgment they are already tried, convicted, and sentenced. You don't know their intentions or their built-in excuses. You simply look at their performance.

Since there are scores of people around the world who read this little column in a multitude of newspapers, magazines, and online publications, it is highly probable that you and I are not personally acquainted; therefore, I can be the one to deliver the harsh news: You are not perfect.

When something goes wrong in your world, it is quite likely that you bear at least some of the responsibility for the outcome. In our lawsuit-happy society, we like to see everything in terms of black and white, assuming that someone else is always at fault. In reality, most errors, arguments, and mistakes are a result of several people's human shortcomings, including yours.

As you go through your day today, when there are problems or criticisms, don't look for excuses or someone else to blame. Consider it an opportunity to examine your own performance and how you can improve.

Today's the day!

THE ULTIMATE CLASSROOM

YOU HAVE PROBABLY HEARD IT SAID THAT SOMEONE ATTENDED the "school of hard knocks." This, of course, means that they may not have had any formal education, but they learned a lot from living their life.

Life is, in fact, the best teacher any of us will ever have. Our past is the lesson, our present is the exam, and our future will be the grades we receive. If we do not learn from the mistakes we have made in the past, we will fail the exam, and our future will be the same as our past. Just like in school, those who do not learn the lessons have to repeat a grade over and over again.

It has been said that the definition of insanity is to continue doing the same thing while expecting a different result. If you make a mistake, it can either be the end of your efforts or the fertilizer that will make your dreams grow in the future.

Studying history is as much about where we are going as where we have been. Those who do not learn from history are destined to repeat it. I am a big fan of my fellow Oklahoman Will Rogers. He wrote many extremely timely newspaper columns and editorials during the 1920s and early 1930s. He was one of the most respected minds and voices of his time. But maybe the most significant thing about Will Rogers' commentaries is that so many of them are still valid and speak to us today.

If you look back at any point in history, you will find that people were struggling with the same things that you and I struggle with today. We have a number of new technological advances that make our lives faster and more convenient, but the issues facing humanity remain the same. A wise person learns from their own mistakes. An even wiser person will learn from the mistakes of others without having to go through the experience themselves.

If you watch professional golfers, either on television or in person, you will see that they observe the line and breaks on the green as other golfers are putting. This is known as "going to school" on the other golfers. We need to do this in our own personal and professional lives. Human beings are unique in that we can build on one another's accomplishments and learn from one another's mistakes.

As you go through your day today, turn mistakes into lessons and lessons into future success.

Today's the day!

CREATING OVERACHIEVERS

IN OUR SOCIETY, THERE IS A CONSTANT, NEVER-ENDING STRUG-gle for normalcy. We seek to fit in at all costs. The advertisers tell us what we should look like, feel like, and smell like, and there is not enough of a premium placed on becoming outstanding.

When we study the lives of overachievers, we find that many of them were faced with a disadvantage or a disability of some type that made it harder for them to be considered normal.

In most cases, these overachievers were simply working harder than the rest of the world to be considered normal. But a funny thing happened to these overachievers on their way to normality. It is called greatness.

It is important for us to understand that greatness comes not from being ten times better than anyone else, or even twice as good. It comes when we are willing to invest just a little more of ourselves toward the task at hand.

If you were to study the biographies of the great overachievers in history, you would find that each of them had a turning point in their lives where they veered off from what we call "average" and became great. In most cases, this turning point comes in the form of a disappointment, a disadvantage, or a disability.

The next time you are faced with a difficult challenge in your life, try viewing it as one of these turning points that can put you on the path toward the greatness for which you have been destined.

In the Chinese language, symbols are used to express thoughts and ideas, and not just individual words. The symbol for crisis has long been identified with the ancient Chinese mariners who viewed crisis as "opportunity on a dangerous wind." The same stormy seas that threaten to founder our ship can often propel us toward a Promised Land that we never before imagined.

Today's the day!

PERSISTENCE AND PROCRASTINATION

DOWN THE STREET FROM MY OFFICE IS A VERY LARGE MEDIA complex containing a TV station, several radio stations, and a large conference center. At one corner of the massive building, there is a large fenced area where several radio and TV broadcast towers soar hundreds of feet into the air. Thousands of people drive by this complex every day and have seen the towers so many times they don't even notice them anymore.

Several months ago, a troubled young man—for reasons of his own—decided to scale the fence and began climbing one of the towers. By the time anyone noticed this young man perched on a precarious ladder hundreds of feet in the air, it was too late to stop him. Police, ambulances, and emergency rescue workers were called to the scene and began efforts to persuade the young man to climb down from the tower.

The young man either ignored them or periodically threatened to jump. As will happen with any large gathering, the media was soon on the scene. TV, radio, and newspaper reporters began around the clock reporting of the ongoing activities of the young man who became known as The Tower Guy.

This went on for days and, somehow, the reporters found things to talk about. The young man became dehydrated, sunburned, and appeared to be disoriented. Finally, one heroic rescue worker was able to communicate with the young man and talk him into coming down.

The final media reports described how persistent The Tower Guy was in remaining on his perch for many days. It's important that we don't confuse persistence with procrastination. It is easy to think that persistence is doing something repeatedly or constantly while procrastination might be thought of as doing nothing at all. In reality, too many of us are like The Tower Guy in that we persist in doing nothing of importance which, in reality, is procrastination as it relates to the things in life we know we should be doing.

Practice does not make perfect, in spite of the old adage. Practice makes consistent. Only perfect practice will make something perfect. Persistence is only a virtue if we are persisting at doing things that matter to us and make the world a better place.

Most people perform activities today because they performed the same activities yesterday and will do it all over again tomorrow. Before you do anything as a regimented part of a routine, make sure you know why you are doing it, what it will accomplish, and when you will be done.

As you go through your day today, make sure you're investing every moment wisely and not just repeating mindless activities because that's what you've always done.

Today's the day!

THE VALUE OF WEALTH

PRICE VS. VALUE

IN OUR SOCIETY TODAY, WE KNOW THE PRICE OF EVERYTHING and the value of virtually nothing. The old adage is true. The best things in life are, indeed, free—or at least free of monetary cost. Warren Buffet said, "Price is what you pay. Value is what you get."

Money is only useful in the areas where money is effective. When it comes to your health, your family, your friends, your faith, and your freedom, money won't solve your problems.

I have been rich and I have been poor, and—all things being equal—rich is certainly better; however, wealth does not make you happy. Wealth simply makes you wealthy. Happiness makes you happy. This is a state of mind and a decision often based on intangibles in our world that are not affected by money. If money is used properly, it can create great value in your life and in the lives of others; however if money is misused, it will take you farther away from the values that will truly make you happy.

Many people in our society are suffering from a disease I call "more." This disease causes you to want more of everything. Unfortunately, the more you get—if you are suffering from this disease—the more you want. You want bigger houses, more expensive cars, designer clothes, and all of the trappings that we are sold minute-by-minute by countless advertising messages. While these things are nice and there's certainly nothing wrong with them, people suffering from the disease of "more," spend money they don't have to buy things they don't need to impress people who don't care. The more they get, the more they want, and in our credit-laden society, these people are getting deeper and deeper into debt, which creates a cycle that takes them farther away from the personal satisfaction and peace that is the basis of true happiness.

It is a fortunate person, indeed, who can manage his or her personal success while experiencing financial success. Any problem that can be solved with money is not really a problem. It's a situation that must be dealt with. I don't ever want to minimize the financial struggles many people are facing; however, we must remember that money is a result. If you can get to the root cause of the problem, the money situation will resolve itself.

As you go through your day today, remember that the price of happiness cannot be paid with money.

Today's the day!

BEING, DOING, AND HAVING

WE LIVE IN A WORLD THAT IS OBSESSED WITH HAVING MORE things. One of the fastest growing industries in our society is the storage business. We are buying so much stuff we can't hold it all.

We have to rent places to put our stuff. There is nothing wrong with having things as long as the things don't really have you.

Unfortunately, we have a preoccupation with buying things that we can't afford, using money we don't have, to impress people who don't care—mentioned in the previous article but worth mentioning again. Acquiring wealth and assets is a by-product of doing work that creates value in the lives of others. In our consumer "buy-now world," we have it backward. We want to have things that will make others think we are already successful.

The universe is set up with three natural steps to success: being, doing, and having. First, you have to "be" the right kind of person who has the motivation, intensity, ethics, and values that would make you successful. Then, after you become this kind of person, you are ready, willing, and able to "do" the things you know are necessary to make you successful. And finally, after you have become the kind of person who is doing the right things, you will inevitably "have" all the stuff and things you want.

In proper balance and as a reward for hard work, having nice things is wonderful. As a facade of smoke and mirrors using consumer credit to create the illusion of success, it is a hollow existence. Trying to have the result first is like the person who stands in front of the fireplace saying, "Give me some heat, and then I will throw in some wood." Or the farmer who says to the field, "Give me a crop, and then I will plow, plant, and fertilize."

When you get the natural system out of order and want to have things before you become the person who would do the right things, you inevitably will still have to pay the price for those things; and if you do it out of order, the price will come attached to a staggering interest charge.

As you go through your day today, focus on yourself as the ultimate tool that will perform the tasks creating value in our world that will inevitably result in you having everything you want and more to share with others around you.

Today's the day!

PAYCHECK TO PAYCHECK

RECENT GOVERNMENT AND INDUSTRY STATISTICS SHOW THAT 70 percent of Americans are living paycheck to paycheck. This means that these individuals are literally less than a month from going into default on their obligations, and bankruptcy is not far behind. When you study the individuals who make up this 70 percent segment of our population, there are some interesting factors that I believe can teach us all some valuable lessons.

The majority of the population who is living paycheck to paycheck have received several raises over the past five years. When you track their earning vs. spending, these raises make little or no long-term difference. In fact, in many cases, these paycheck to paycheck individuals are actually worse off financially several months after receiving an increase in income. This is because they use their increased income to secure more consumer debt.

This consumer debt, quite often, is used to purchase things that are decreasing in value. Any time you are involved in an economic model that involves borrowing money, paying a high rate of interest, and acquiring assets that are not worth the amount of the obligation while they continue to go down in value, you are in a never-ending losing cycle.

If you are one of these paycheck to paycheck individuals who makes up 70 percent of our population, let's look at some steps you can take to break the cycle.

1. Stop all consumer debt going forward. If you find yourself in a hole, literally or figuratively, the first step toward getting out of the hole is to stop digging. Cut up your credit cards and vow to never again buy anything involving consumer debt.

2. Give your household a thorough financial checkup. Figure out how much money is coming in and where it is all going. You will be amazed at the amount of money you spend on things you had never really considered. I'm not telling you how you should spend your money, I'm simply saying it should be a conscious decision on your part. You work hard for your money, and it should work hard for you in the areas where you want to spend your income.

3. Get on a budget. A budget is nothing more or less than you taking control and ordering your money to do what you want it to do. Your budget is not a confining, inflexible document. Instead, it is there to help you save your sinking financial ship.

If you will follow these three simple steps, you will find yourself in the upper 30 percent of people in our society and well on your way to financial independence.

As you go through your day today, remember you're going to have to change your financial pattern if you're going to change your financial results.

Today's the day!

RAIN OR SHINE

A WISE MAN ONCE TOLD ME, "PEOPLE WHO THINK THAT IT IS never going to rain again are destined to get very wet." Whether it's the stock market, your health, the weather, or the economic conditions, change is inevitable. Success lies in creating a balance between planning for the best and preparing for the worst. There are some people who base everything in their personal and professional lives on a best-case scenario. Any minor bump in the road can cause these people to have a fatal crash. On the other hand, there are people who spend so much time planning for the proverbial rainy day that they never enjoy the sunshine.

Recently, I enjoyed a conference championship basketball game. One team was heavily favored, and they were way ahead with less than five minutes to go in the game. Their coach called time out and obviously changed their game plan. When they came back out on the floor, they held the ball and stalled for time trying to run out the clock. Unfortunately for them, this talented team was great at shooting and scoring but was not good at this delay tactic. They turned the ball over to the other team a number of times and lost the game in overtime. It could be said that they became a victim of their own caution.

On the other hand, often a reasonable degree of caution can be an investment of a few pennies for a return of many dollars. Recently, we installed a new computer system in our office. I will not bore you with the details as it would become immediately apparent that I know nothing about computers. The one important factor I do understand about this new computer is the dual safety backup system. For a relatively modest cost, we can protect ourselves against losing information worth many thousands of dollars if, indeed, the information could even be replaced at all. In all situations we must weigh both the risk and the reward.

Sometimes, the choices can be literally life and death. This year I have realized one of my long-term goals as we are traveling for a number of my events in a private plane. When making arrangements for our first trip, I noticed all of the expenses itemized in the contract. It listed fuel, airport charges, and the pilot's fee. When I inquired about the cost of the co-pilot, I was told that they generally don't provide one on private flights. When I found out the cost for the co-pilot was approximately $200, which represents a tiny fraction of the expense of traveling in a private plane, I let them know that I would always be traveling with a co-pilot. While the risk may be small, the consequences are permanent.

As you go through your day today, look for ways to both plan for the best and prepare for the worst.

Today's the day!

MAGIC MONEY

THERE ARE FEW THINGS IN OUR CHAOTIC LIVES THAT ARE MORE reliable and dependable than money. Dollars can be counted, budgeted, and allocated. Money acts the same way every time and will do exactly what you tell it to do, but it's not magic. I'm always amazed when people take this down-to-earth medium of exchange and expect it to be magical.

For over 25 years, I have had a college scholarship, and to date, we have helped send more than 500 students to my alma mater. Recently, I ran into an aspiring student and her mother at an event where I was speaking, and they told me they were hoping to get one of my scholarships. When I told them we were going to have a board meeting to review the scholarships in just a few days, they were astonished and replied, "Oh, we didn't fill out an application."

I am baffled how often people expect their bills to be paid, retirement to be established, and expenses to be handled through some magical property of money that simply doesn't exist. If you're depending on money to do something that can't be added up, multiplied, or compounded, it's probably not going to happen. People are invariably waiting for their ship to come in, and the majority of them never sent a ship out.

A significant percentage of people who have access to free matching dollars for their retirement funds through their employer still don't take advantage of it. People who attend my Millionaire Institute events learn that if you will save $10 a day and invest in a simple Index Fund that has returned 12 percent for more than half a century, you will be a millionaire in 30 years. People are astonished when they see the simple mathematics, but when I follow up to see how many of them are saving $10 a day, I am generally disappointed by people's failure to engage.

Money is a great tool if you use it, and a tremendous slave if you put it to work. Money is the fuel that can make your dreams come true, but they will always be just dreams if you don't put the fuel in the engine and engage the ignition switch. To end up where you want to be, you've got to go on a journey from here to there, and to have a successful journey, you've got to start.

Financial independence is within your reality once you give up the myth of magical money.

As you go through your day today, live in the real world, not in the smoke and mirrors of magical money.

Today's the day!

THE MONEY RULES

THERE'S PROBABLY NOTHING MORE MISUNDERSTOOD IN OUR society than the acquisition and use of money. Nothing can take the place of money in the things that money does, but outside of the small scope where money is useful, it has little or no value. When it comes to your health, family relationships, or personal well-being, money is of little importance.

It is fascinating to me that we can go through twelve years of public education, and many of us acquire university degrees, but we have received little or no training in how to deal with the commodity that is our universal means of exchange. There are probably more books and seminars on the subject of money, but still the mystery persists.

There are only four things you can do with your money: acquire stuff, buy security, create memories, and make the world a better place. There is no right or wrong place to put your money as it relates to these four areas. As in most life decisions, balance is the key.

Acquiring "stuff" has become our national pastime and obsession. Most people spend more time working than necessary so they can acquire stuff that they don't have time to use because they spend so much time working to get it. Security is an admirable pursuit. But if you're not careful, you will fall into the group of people who spend their whole lives preparing for a rainy day, and it never so much as sprinkles. Creating memories is an important activity. Those memories can never be taken from you, but if all you do is pursue memories, you will spend your entire life looking in the rear view mirror. It's nice to look back there every once in a while, but if you drive through life very long looking in the rear view mirror, you are bound to get a rude awakening.

And, finally, money—like any other tool—can be used for good or for bad, but it can, indeed, help to make the world a better place when it is put in the hands of the right people. We must be cautious here as well, because among those sincere souls who seek your money for admirable pursuits, there are many who—under the guise of good works—are prepared to rip you off.

Make up your mind to spend your money wisely, because at the end of the day, what you buy with your money better be worth it to you, because you invested one day of your life to get it.

Today's the day!

THE 1 PERCENT

IN RECENT MONTHS AND YEARS, THERE HAVE BEEN NUMEROUS protests and debates regarding the richest 1 percent of our population. I have never seen a group so maligned that so many people want to join. You need look no farther than the lines to buy lottery tickets when the jackpot grows into the mega millions.

At the recent World Economic Forum, projections were revealed stating that by 2016, over half the world's wealth will be in the hands of 1 percent of the population. The rich are getting richer, and the poor are getting poorer. I will leave it to politicians, economists, and pundits to debate whether this is good or bad, but for you and me, it is simply a reality.

Weather forecasters might disagree on how cold an upcoming winter will be, but as winter approaches, it behooves us all to get out our heavy coats. As always, the burning question is not what happens on Wall Street or at the White House. The question is what happens on your street and in your house. The growing disparity among people's income and wealth is inevitable. It is left to you and me to decide which way we want to go as we are forced off of the fence.

I have been poorer than most of my readers who get these weekly columns, and today I have thankfully achieved a level of wealth that few people approach. Wealth does not make you better, happier, or more significant. It does make you more of whatever you are. If you are a kind and generous person, wealth will bring you the resources to spread your kindness and generosity. If you are a self-serving or self-destructive person, wealth will make you able to hurt others and destroy yourself even faster.

If you want to join the 1 percent, you should not do what they do, but instead, do what they did when they began. The most certain way to insure you will never be a person of wealth is to try to act like you already are. Creating wealth is a simple equation of spending less than you earn. Those who succeed most dramatically work on both sides of this equation to enhance their earning and control their spending.

Millionaires have different attitudes and perceptions than the 99 percent. If you would like to take a millionaire profile and get a free assessment to see how you stack up, you can find it at www.TheMillionaireMap.com.

You can have a very successful and fulfilled life and be among the 99 percent if you plan, save, and invest properly. You can join the 1 percent if you focus and strive in measured and consistent ways. Either course is acceptable depending upon your goals and aspirations, but as the world economic conditions tighten and the rich do, indeed, get richer as the poor get poorer, you need to have a specific plan to succeed going one way or the other.

Don't be like the squirrel in the middle of the road as the truck approaches. Going either way will work. Not having a plan and staying where you are will get you financially killed. As you go through your day today, make your money a tool and not a goal, whether you're in the 1 percent or the 99 percent.

Today's the day!

A LOOK AT LEGACY

THE IRON LADY

I REMEMBER A TIME IN MY LIFE—IRONICALLY BEFORE LOSING my sight—that I rarely, if ever, read an entire book cover to cover. As an author today of over 30 titles with more than 10 million books in print, I'm not proud to have to admit that when I could read with my eyes as you are reading these words on the page of a book or on your computer screen through an online publication, I wasn't even a casual reader. Today, thanks to high-speed audio books, I read virtually an entire book every day. This has been my habit now for more than 20 years, so I have completed roughly 7,000 books.

Among these are many biographies of historical figures I admire. One such leader I have come to respect as much as anyone I have ever studied is Margaret Thatcher. She led her country vigorously through some very difficult times. She excelled under conditions that would have been difficult for any man and virtually impossible for a woman given the obstacles she had to deal with.

I came to have an interest in Margaret Thatcher when I began studying about Ronald Reagan, and he described the respect and admiration he had for Mrs. Thatcher. Reagan, who justifiably became known as the Great Communicator, respected Margaret Thatcher for her ability to express an entire concept within one simple phrase. One such phrase often repeated by Margaret Thatcher was, "Socialism is a wonderful thing until you run out of other people's money to spend."

Socialism is a misunderstood and deceptive concept. At first glance, it would appear to be both practical and admirable. Why can't we all just simply do our best and share equally in the rewards? It's a beautiful idea except for one simple fact— socialism doesn't work. For the same reason that no one ever washed a rental car or made the bed in their hotel room, socialism is a bankrupt philosophy.

If you want to get something done, put someone in charge of it, and incentivize them to complete the task. If you want to get it done better and faster, offer them a bonus.

The pilgrims who settled North America nearly starved to death when they practiced collective farming, but then, as a last-ditch effort, they divided the land equally and let everyone cultivate their own crops. The result was an overwhelming success and a surplus from their harvest.

My friend and mentor, Steve Forbes, in his book *How Capitalism Will Save Us,* explained that the best way to get resources to those deemed to be less fortunate is to allow those who can excel to do so and then benevolently provide for those around them. If you don't believe this works, just drive through your own town or city and look at the number of hospitals, libraries, parks, and schools that bear the names of successful capitalists. Please let me know if you ever find any such example of generosity given by a socialist.

As you go through your day today, remember Margaret Thatcher, and serve, prosper, and share.

Today's the day!

MONEY MORONS

REASONABLE PEOPLE CAN DISAGREE ON BOTH METHODS AND missions. I'm a firm believer that there are at least two sides to every argument, and virtually all opinions have some merit; however, occasionally, you hear an otherwise-intelligent human being utter a phrase that is so nonsensical and out of touch with reality it's virtually impossible to overlook.

Recently I was in Las Vegas conducting a three-day event called The Millionaire Institute based on my recent book, *The Millionaire Map*. People flew in from across the country and, literally, around the world, to hear me give fourteen hours of training over three days on building wealth. Because I had been teaching intensely and nonstop throughout the weekend, I was probably more in tune with financial and money matters than I would have otherwise been.

When my colleague and I arrived at the airport in Las Vegas for our flight home, we were confronted with row upon row of slot machines extending right up to the point where passengers go through the security check. There was a young couple arguing so frantically and loudly that those of us in the security line could not help but overhear. The 20-something-year-old young woman said emphatically, "We've got to go right now or we're going to miss our plane." The young man responded, as if he didn't have a care in the world, with a phrase I think I shall never forget. "Just be patient; it won't take me more than a few minutes to lose the rest of our money." He proceeded to methodically put the rest of their money into a slot machine.

As I cleared security, I remember thinking, *On what planet does that phrase even begin to make sense?* However, the insanity is not confined to young couples determined to throw away their hard-earned money in Las Vegas.

For years, my company, the Narrative Television Network, has done business with the federal government. Your Uncle Sam makes a very interesting and complicated customer. Due to our federal contracts, I am required to attend periodic meetings in Washington, DC, for contractors and companies who supply goods and services for the United States government and its various federal programs.

I actually sat in a meeting in which a gentleman who works with the General Accounting Office addressed hundreds of businesspeople who supply the government. He said unequivocally, "We have far too many new contractors who have a project gap and a program fund balance." I did not know what a project gap or a program fund balance was, but the government official explained it in such a way I knew it was bad.

Later, I had the opportunity to ask this gentleman to define a project gap and program fund balance. He explained it in such a way that I came to understand that to those of us in the real world known as the private sector, he was lamenting hardworking individuals who had delivered their contracted products or services ahead of time and under budget. Only in dealing with the federal government could these admirable qualities be deemed as a bad outcome.

When you find someone who's a little off course or misguided, it's good to point out the error of their ways, and help them; but when you confront these types of statements that are pure insanity, there is no comment necessary. You just tuck them away for future reference to inspire, motivate, and amuse.

As you go through your day today, help everyone you can, and isolate everyone you can't.

Today's the day!

FAMILY MATTERS

THIS PAST WEEKEND, I UNDERTOOK THE ANNUAL PILGRIMAGE to a neighboring state where I attended my family reunion. This yearly event has become somewhat of a regular parentheses in my personal and professional life. It is a time to escape my normal routine and consider the past, reevaluate the present, and contemplate the future.

My family is probably much like yours in that my ancestors ran the gambit of the human experience; therefore, to paraphrase Dickens, family histories can be the best of times and the worst of times. This year, one of my relatives conducted some impressive research and gave a report on a book she had compiled of our family's history over the past three or four centuries. It was intriguing to consider that ancestors who populate my family tree distinguished themselves in all manner of pursuits including public service, business, ministry, and train robbery among many others.

It was Gandhi who gave us the enduring wisdom that every person is our superior in that we can learn something from them. Sometimes we learn things we want to emulate, and other times we learn things we want to avoid. I treasure the time I get to spend with my family and try to stay connected with them throughout the year as much as possible—more for my own personal enjoyment than from any sense of duty.

The four generations that were represented at this year's gathering are a quality group of people I am proud to be a part of. Some of the individuals I am directly related to, and others are just friends who have attached themselves to our family. In any event, they are all tremendous assets in my life.

In my book *The Ultimate Gift* and the movie based upon it, I described a dysfunctional family trying to rectify the problems from the past. In the chapter entitled The Gift of Family, I gave my own definition: *"Some people are born into wonderful families. Others have to find or create them. Being a member of a family is a priceless privilege which costs nothing but love."*

Here in the 21ˢᵗ century, while it's easier to stay in touch with family members, we are in danger of losing some of the archives and records upon which future generations will depend. If you have family photos, correspondence, or other printed material, be sure to preserve it digitally and back it up in several places. While your most senior generation is alive and well, have them identify the people, places, and things in photos and family videos. Someday there will be no one around to identify those elements that have gone before.

If you think about an immediate or distant family member throughout the day, and you're trying to decide whether you should contact them, the answer is always yes.

As you go through your day today, think of your family as a treasure, and treat them that way.

Today's the day!

TRUTH ABOUT INVESTING

I HAVE HAD THE PRIVILEGE OF WRITING A WEEKLY COLUMN almost 500 times over the past ten years. It is regularly read in newspapers, magazines, and online publications by millions of people literally around the world. From time to time, I send out a challenge to readers via my weekly effort.

Several times over the previous decade, I have questioned the wisdom and validity of those brave and brash individuals who purport to succeed at timing the stock market. Timing the market is the long-touted practice of using charts, graphs, tea leaves, or phases of the moon to determine the exact moment to get in and out of the market, thereby getting rich while those timid souls who just stay in the market only get a 10 or 12 percent return year after year.

First, let me state as a mathematical fact that consistent, regular investment into the average return of the stock market will inevitably make an individual financially successful. Although there may be better ways to invest, simply putting a few hundred dollars each month into an index fund that buys a piece of every stock in the marketplace, historically will return between 10 and 12 percent, and this is more than enough to reach your financial goals. Don't take my word for it. Break out your pocket calculator and get ready to be astounded by the miracle of compounded returns on consistent investments.

Assuming that my best effort to get you to be an investor like the proverbial tortoise instead of the hare has failed, and you are going to be the next mega-millionaire, day trader, or market timer, let's look at the facts.

My friend and broker, Matt Monger at Merrill Lynch, provided me with some actual market statistics showing that, over a 20-year period, the average market trader or timer actually lost 3.29 percent per year while the market as a whole over the same period went up 12.98 percent. Statistics don't lie, even if some people trying to sell computerized trading software on late night cable TV do.

If we were talking about the crab grass in your yard or your necktie being out of style, I wouldn't worry about these false notions, but the returns on your hard-earned dollars represent your financial future and your dreams.

As you go through your day today, remember, a boring investment portfolio can give you an exciting life while an exciting portfolio may give you a boring life.

Today's the day!

Driving Your Money

AMONG THE MOST PROFOUND PHILOSOPHERS AND COLUM-nists of the 20th century was Will Rogers. People waited each day to learn what Will would write in the newspaper or say on the radio. During the depths of the Depression, he announced, "America will go down in history as the only nation that will go to the poor house in an automobile." That was true then and maybe even more profound today.

The average car payment in America is approaching $400 per month over 72 months. This virtually insures that most of the cars driving on the highway will never be paid off. There will be a remaining balance when that car is traded in on a new one, and the remaining debt is rolled into a new loan. When you consider that cars are the most expensive things we buy that go down in value, this is a recipe for disaster.

When you study millionaires, you find that—on aver-age—they drive a two- to three-year-old car and keep it for a number of years. Paying cash for a two- to three-year-old car allows you to enjoy a very nice automobile while letting some-one else take the depreciation hit that happens within the first few years after a car drives away from the show room.

If the average car payment, $400 per month, were invested over a working lifetime, you, your children, and grandchildren could be financially independent. If you can ever get to the point where you make that last payment on your car, don't consider it the end but consider it the beginning. Continue to drive that car and continue to make the monthly payment, but instead of paying the finance company, pay yourself. Within a few short years, you will have the ability to act like the average millionaire in our society when you walk onto a car lot and pay cash for your next automobile.

If you will continue making these payments to yourself instead of making the payments plus interest to the bank, you will be on your way to financial success. Don't buy into the myth that you have to have a car payment for your entire life.

We are bombarded with car ads offering us easy terms, no money down, and liberal trade-in opportunities. If it seems like this is a great deal, it is, but only if you're a bank or automobile finance company. Nothing rides better than a paid-for car.

As you go through your day today, think of your car in terms of your long-term financial planning and not your response to a short-term TV ad.

Today's the day!

WALL STREET ON SALE

I AM CERTAINLY NOT THE FIRST TO TELL YOU THAT THE WAY TO make money in the stock market is to buy low and sell high. As ridiculously simple as this seems, the majority of individual investors make a habit of buying high and selling low. This is because they invest with their hearts and not with their heads.

You can visualize the stock market by picturing a young boy walking upstairs playing with a yo-yo. If you focus on the boy ascending the stairs, you will be very comfortable. If you focus, however, on the quick, abrupt drops of the yo-yo, you will panic.

Everyone seems to have a good attitude when the market is up, but to an average individual investor, a down market signals distress, depression, and doom. To the successful, long-term investor, a down market signals a buying opportunity. It's like going to the mall when everything is on sale. When you consider these buying opportunities, it is realistic to think that you make money when you buy and not just when you sell.

There are a few things to keep in mind if you are going to invest in the stock market.

1. Diversify. You must own a wide number of stocks from a diverse number of industries. If you put all your eggs in one basket, you may do well this month and this year, but you are a disaster waiting to happen. There are a number of index funds and mutual funds for small investors that do not have the resources to diversify on their own.

2. Have a long-term horizon. If you cannot invest your money for more than five years, do not invest in the stock market. Remember the boy with the yo-yo. Over a five-year period or longer, it's easy to have results that look like the boy climbing the stairs; however, if you have a short-term horizon, it is likely your results will look like the yo-yo when the bottom drops out.

3. Invest regularly. Most investors succeed when they have a systematic, automatic, regular investment plan. They put money into selected investments at the same time each month or each quarter. This makes it more likely you will be investing with your head and not your heart.

4. Don't get married to any single investment. Remember, we want to buy low and sell high—not buy low, watch it get high, and then become low again. When you buy a stock, you should already have your sell point in mind. Look at everything in your portfolio and consider if you didn't own it,

would you buy it. If the answer is not an emphatic "Yes," sell today.

As you go through your day today, look at your investments as a long-term vehicle taking you toward your dreams. Short-term drops in the market simply signal a blue-light special.

Today's the day!

THE DEBT DILEMMA

WHETHER IT'S COLLEGE LOANS, CAR LOANS, HOME MORTGAGES, or month-to-month consumer credit, people in our society are convinced that debt is a normal part of life.

Our parents and grandparents grew up with the attitude that if you can't afford it now, what makes you think that you can afford it later? We have been sold and have come to believe—hook, line, and sinker—that we should not wait. Instead, we can have it now and pay for it later. Unfortunately for too many, later never comes or it dawns on us at a point far beyond our ability to recover.

It's important to realize that no one got over their head in debt overnight. You didn't fall down a well. You started a gradual decline down an extremely slippery slope. Unfortunately, this debt slope is very deceiving. It is much like riding a bicycle down a long, gradual incline. You barely notice you're going downhill until you turn around and try to peddle back up the hill.

There are a few things you should do once you recognize you are in trouble with respect to credit. But first, you must recognize you are in trouble. If you are experiencing any of the following symptoms, you want to act immediately:

1. You cannot pay all of your consumer credit such as credit cards, unsecured loans, etc. in full each month.

2. You are late in paying any of your regular bills that maintain your lifestyle such as your home mortgage, utilities, or insurance.

3. You are taking out additional lines of credit or credit cards to pay off existing bills.

4. You run out of money long before you run out of month.

5. There have been any negative changes in your income or expenses due to job loss, illness, or other unforeseen factors.

The sooner you can identify the fact that you're having a credit crisis, the easier the problem is to resolve. Don't wait until you're neck deep in debt. As soon as you realize there is an unhealthy trend, act, and do the following:

1. Declare financial marshal law, and do not spend any money that does not maintain or improve your situation.

2. Compile a written budget that shows where your money went over the past few months and where you intend it to go over the coming months.

3. Contact your creditors and let them know you are having some issues, why you are having issues, and what they can expect.

4. Commit yourself to slowly getting out of the hole and further commit to never getting in a hole again.

5. Establish an emergency fund of at least six months of your normal expenditures. It's going to rain again. Don't get caught without an umbrella.

As you go through your day today, be sure to control your debt instead of allowing your debt to control you.

Today's the day!

LEARNING IS A LIFELONG PROCESS

THE AGE OF KNOWLEDGE

THERE ARE A NUMBER OF PERIODS IN HISTORY THAT ARE CON-sidered to have been times of great knowledge and enlightenment. There are a handful of historical figures we consider to be the greatest minds of their time or even all times. We think of Albert Einstein, Leonardo DaVinci, and Thomas Edison among the greatest thinkers and innovators of the times in which they lived.

With regard to sheer knowledge, information, and potential expertise, these amazing people and hundreds of others collectively would be envious of you. Any high school student of average intelligence in the 21st century with a computer, Internet access, and a search engine, would be considered beyond a mega-genius at any time in recorded history.

If you are over 40 years of age, you remember a time when, if you wanted to know something, you had to go to a library, call someone, or consult your family's Encyclopedia to even obtain a small amount of information. Now if you want to know who pitched the third game of the World Series in 1937 or how many long horn cattle there are in Arkansas or how much tea there actually is in China, all you need do is go to the nearest computer or smart phone, type in a few brief commands, and there it is.

Knowledge is the beginning of all good things we can have in life. Ignorance is the curse that keeps people from these good things. There is no excuse in the 21st century for being ignorant. I have heard people say, "I don't know how to use a computer" or "I don't have access to the Internet." You are currently reading a column written by a guy who cannot physically read a computer screen and does not know how to type on a computer keyboard. Nevertheless, I regularly tap into endless knowledge through the Internet with a little help from my colleagues.

Curiosity for most thinking people who have ever lived on earth was a natural, ongoing state. It was normal for people to think and even say, "I've always wondered…." In the past, people heard their parents and grandparents curiously remark, "I wonder…." Generations of people heard the question but simply did not have access to the answer. We live in a world today where the rules have changed. People who will prosper play by the new rules. If you believe that the winners are the people who get the most, you must understand that the people who get the most know the most.

As you go through your day today, commit to no longer idly wondering about things. Find the answers, realize that these answers will lead you to more questions, and know that those questions will lead you to your destiny.

Today's the day!

THE TWELVE BOOK RULE

HERE IN THE 21ST CENTURY, WE DON'T GET COMPENSATED FOR how hard we work. We get compensated for how much we know. Becoming an expert on even a very small thing is generally better than having some basic knowledge of a lot of things. A brain surgeon may not know how to change his oil, turn on his vacuum, balance his check book, or run a washing machine. The brain surgeon may know very little about virtually everything, but if he or she knows virtually everything about brain surgery, that person will probably have a profitable, satisfying, and fulfilling life.

It is a fascinating study to contemplate how much you need to know to be considered an expert in a given field. Our brain surgeon went to school, studied, and interned for over a decade.

Most things in life do not involve this level of concentrated expertise. You may know absolutely nothing about actuarial tables, natural gas reserves, lift coefficients, major league batting averages, or cake recipes. It is fascinating to talk with people who are experts in these areas and many others and ask them how many text books or resources they have really mastered in order to be considered an expert.

Most people would be surprised to know that in many endeavors of life, the right twelve books will put you into an elite category of knowledge. In many fields, you don't even have to have elite knowledge. You simply need to know a little more than the average person on the street. Be sure if you're going to study in a certain field to become an expert that you're studying the right books.

The right books are defined and determined only by the top experts in a field. In order to find these books, you've got to talk to the experts. In order to find the experts, you've got to ask other experts. If you inquire of many people, they will lead you to believe they are an expert or a top performer in their field. This may or may not be true; however, if instead you ask someone in a field who they think the top experts are, you will begin to get many of the same names. And lo and behold, you will find a short list of experts. If you call a handful of these people and ask them for a list of books or resources you should read, you will compile an amazing list. If you read one of these books each month for a year, you will quite likely be an expert within most any field you choose.

As you go through your day today, decide what area you want to master. Read what the experts in that field read, and shortly you will not be talking to the experts, you will be an expert.

Today's the day!

Trying and Doing

Just because you can do something doesn't mean you should, and just because you can't do something doesn't mean you shouldn't.

We need to define ourselves based on the decisions we make to do or not do things that correspond to our goals and aspirations. If there's something you do not want to do, and it does not adversely define who you are, you can put it behind you and go on with your life.

I have written more than 30 books, worked on four screenplays from my novels that were turned into movies, and written almost a thousand weekly columns. Ironically, I don't know how to type. After losing my sight, I tried briefly to master the typing skill, but I quickly discovered, as a former Olympic weightlifting champion, my hands didn't seem to be made for a computer keyboard.

My weekly columns, as well as all of my books and screenplays, are efficiently typed, meticulously proofed, and masterfully edited by my friend and colleague Dorothy Thompson. I could have labored for a decade to improve my typing skills, and I would not have approached the level where Dorothy effortlessly performs.

Deciding I did not want to type has not kept me from being a best-selling author with more than 10 million books in print; however, about the same time I made my efforts toward exploring becoming a typist, I encountered a challenge with a mailbox near my office. Our office is on a busy street that is a main thoroughfare in the city where I live and work. The mailbox we used at that time was located about three or four hundred yards along that street, requiring anyone walking to that mailbox to cross a side street and traverse a busy parking lot. One day everyone in the office was busy, and we had some correspondence that had to get in the mailbox. I scooped up the mail and headed for the mailbox only to discover, given the traffic noise, street to cross, and congested parking lot, I couldn't do it. I dejectedly returned to my office with the out-going mail still in my hand.

I would be the first to admit that it is not imperative that a successful CEO of a television network be able or even willing to take the mail to the mailbox, but it began to bother me, and in my own mind, going through the mail each day was a con-stant reminder there was something I couldn't do.

My late, great friend and mentor Coach John Wooden told me, "You can choose to do the things you are able to do, but you must do the things you are unable to do if they are limit-ing your progress."

Suffice it to say, through trial, effort, frustration, and tears, I eventually made it to the mailbox one afternoon, dropped off the mail, and got back to my office. I never did it again, and I never needed to do it again. That one trip to the mailbox wasn't about sending the letters out. It was about redefining who I am.

As you go through your day today, never allow yourself to become defined by anything you can't do.

Today's the day!

BUSY IS BETTER

WHEN I WAS A YOUNG PERSON, ONE OF MY MENTORS TOLD ME, "If you want to get something done, ask someone who's already busy to do it." This seemed counterintuitive or even ridiculous to me then. Today, while I can't explain why it works, experience has, indeed, taught me that people who are already getting a lot done seem to be most able to do more.

In a recent study of college students, it was revealed that students who worked a part-time job, up to 20 hours per week in addition to their coursework, actually performed better and got higher grades than students who didn't work at all. There is something about having a lot to do that forces us to both prioritize and focus.

Success is a result of not only doing things right but also doing the right things. People who write things down, keep a detailed calendar, and organize their time function at a higher level while producing more and better results. In much the same way that organized investors get better returns on their money, organized people get better results from their time.

I have written 30 books having sold in excess of 10 million copies. In each of my books, as well as in all of my weekly columns, I provide my contact information. People from around the world call or email me about a variety of questions involving success. Among the most frequently-asked questions I receive is, "How do you get so much done?" I have no definitive answer other than my time is very well organized by an efficient and effective team of professionals.

All of my books and weekly columns, including the words you are reading now, are typed, proofed, and edited by my colleague, Dorothy Thompson. In addition to being the best grammarian and editor in the publishing industry, Dorothy manages my calendar, correspondence, and daily activities. Recently, due to some family health issues and the holiday season, Dorothy was out of the office for almost a full month, only coming in a few hours each week to deal with the most critical matters. Ironically, we found that when she returned to the office fulltime, we were amazingly caught up with all of our tasks, duties, and responsibilities. Without fully intending to do so, we had organized the most critical elements of our work into the most productive activities surrounding those few hours that Dorothy and I could work together.

Unlike most people, as a blind person myself, having my team around me is not simply a convenience. It is a necessity. To this end, my blindness has probably made me more efficient and effective.

I believe each of us can do more with less if we will just focus on the priorities and the possibilities.

As you go through your day today, maximize your minutes with the activities that matter.

Today's the day!

LEARNING ABOUT LEARNING

FOR MORE THAN 25 YEARS, I HAVE PROVIDED SCHOLARSHIPS for young people wanting to attend a private university here in my home town. Over the years, our scholarship fund has assisted more than 500 students with their education. I'm always amazed that young people will make great personal and financial sacrifices to apply to many universities in hopes that they can get a college degree. After being accepted to an institution, they commit a great amount of time and money toward their goal, but they can be heard to ask questions such as, "Are we required to come to class?" and "How much of the book do we have to read?" and "Will this actually be on the test?" They strive to avoid as much of the very classroom that they spent so much time trying to get in to.

The term "school" comes from a Greek word that means "free time." School was actually a reward or an honor that was bestowed upon a young person who didn't have to work in the fields a full day but was allowed to spend some of their time thinking, learning, and becoming exposed to new ideas.

Education is a lifelong process. It does not end when we graduate. Quite the contrary in fact. Our real education begins when we leave school, which is why the graduation ceremony is called a commencement.

I often think we put far too much emphasis on formal education as opposed to informal education. While I am very proud of my university education and degree, most of the things I know today that impact the way I live and pursue my passions came to me after my formal education.

If you read ten books on any subject, you will know more than 99 percent of people on that topic. We all need to organize our informal education as much as our formal education is organized. You need to have a reading list of books, magazines, and newspapers that pertain to your area of interest or passion. If you're not sure what to read and study, simply ask the people who are where you want to be for a reading list.

My late, great friend, colleague, and publisher, Charlie "Tremendous" Jones always said, "You will be the same person you are today five years from now except for the books you read and the people you meet." Through reading books and meeting people, you can go anywhere you want to go, be anything you want to be, and do anything you want to do.

As you go through your day today, commit to learning what you need to know to live the life you want to live.

Today's the day!

READING

MANY PEOPLE ASK ME WHERE TO FIND GREAT WISDOM, KNOWL-edge, information, and the best mentors. This is much simpler than it would appear. The greatest minds and spirits the world has ever known are waiting to help you get from where you are to where you want to be. Whether it's Winston Churchill teaching you about leadership, William Shakespeare discussing beauty, or Albert Einstein commenting on the theory of relativity, they are all as close as your nearest library or bookstore.

As the author of many books, I have worked with a number of people in the publishing industry. David C. Cook published several of my current titles, including a compilation of my weekly columns entitled *Today's the Day*. The President and CEO of David C. Cook is a friend and true leader in the industry, Cris Doornbos. He has lived by a slogan for over 25 years, "Read a book and grow." This is the way to success, both personally and professionally.

The wisdom and knowledge that books offer us can be even greater than what you would have received had you known Churchill, Shakespeare, or Einstein in person. Through books written by them and about them, you can get the condensed wisdom, knowledge, and experience they each accumulated over their entire lifetime.

After losing my sight at the age of 29, I began devouring a book a day, thanks to the National Library for the Blind's special recordings and a high-speed tape player. Reading has changed my life. It has introduced me to the greatest people, places, and events of history, as well as opened the imagination and creativity of the best minds the world has to offer. Reading has brought me far more success and recognition than I deserve and is the single factor that has allowed me to be a successful writer.

A person who doesn't read is no better off than a person who can't read. Literacy is a gift but only if we use it and apply it in real ways in our personal and professional lives. Several years ago, there was an in-depth research study done on the top executives of the Fortune 500 companies. This study sought to determine what attributes these corporate leaders had in common. They explored background, marital status, education, and a variety of other factors. At the end of the study, it was determined that the single element that these Fortune 500 corporate leaders had in common was that they read or listened to motivational, informational, or instructional material on a regular basis.

We live in a world where we are compensated for what we know more than what we do. A person who can do things can always have a job, but a person who knows things can create untold wealth and success. Beyond wealth and success, reading can introduce you to thoughts and ideas that can bring you peace, contentment, joy, and happiness beyond your wildest dreams.

As you go through your day today, find some consistent time to meet the greatest people the world has ever known through books. They are waiting for you and me.

Today's the day!

GETTING IT

ONE OF MY FAVORITE POETS IS ROBERT FROST. I ENJOY HIS poetry, not only because it has the beauty and artistic flavor one should expect from a poet, but it quite often contains a hidden but extremely valuable life lesson. If you haven't read it or even if you haven't read it recently, please read Frost's poem entitled *The Road Less Traveled*. It is an owner's manual for life and a study in wisdom regarding how to make great decisions.

In another work, Frost posed the poignant question, "How many times does something have to happen to you before something occurs to you?" I believe much of our practical learning comes from the disappointment and pain of overcoming our own mistakes. If these mistakes are, indeed, the price of wisdom, we need not pay the bill more often than necessary. All of us know people who, in their personal and professional lives, continue to stand out in the proverbial rain while constantly lamenting the fact that they're getting wet.

In my early childhood and teenage years, I had a dog that was very special to me. My dog was not particularly well-bred or trained, but taught me many lessons. This dog, on one occasion, ran full speed into a glass door. After reviving from semi-consciousness, it went over to the pane of glass and examined it carefully. From that day forward, throughout a decade of remaining life, my dog never again went through that door without first stopping and slowly moving forward until making certain that the glass door was open. We can all learn a lesson from this wise canine—not so much regarding running into glass doors, but with respect to constantly running into the same or similar obstacles in our lives.

You have probably heard the quote, usually attributed to Albert Einstein, that the definition of insanity is continuing to do the same thing while expecting a different result. How many people do you know who go from job to job, relationship to relationship, and investment to investment and continually and consistently meet with disaster? These individuals continue to look around them at other people and situations and believe that their environment is at fault.

You and I are the only consistent factors in every success and failure we have experienced in life. Until we take full responsibility for our mistakes, learn from them, and move forward—not necessarily expecting to be perfect but vowing not to make the same mistakes—we have not yet reached the starting gate for our race toward success.

As you go through your day today, think of the mistakes you have made in the past and look for the lesson. Pain can be a harsh teacher. Let us vow not to be forced to repeat the class.

Today's the day!

MASTER YOUR TIME

TIME BANK

TIME IS THE MOST UNCERTAIN, ELUSIVE, AND MOST PRECIOUS commodity that any of us possess in our personal or professional lives. It is the one true nonrenewable resource. I have read no less than a dozen books on time management, and the truth is we can't manage time. If we are diligent and committed, we may be able to manage ourselves, but time does, indeed, march on.

We live in a society where everyone wants a piece of your time. Fortunately, or unfortunately, you and I spent all of our time yesterday doing something; therefore, if we take on something new today, it will have to replace something else. How we invest our time is a matter of priorities, but we must make sure they're our priorities and not someone else's.

Unfortunately, the utilizations of time that most people would deem to be most important are too often relegated to whatever time may be left over. Most people would consider family time, study time, recreational time, and personal development time to be times they want to make higher priorities in the future. These things are too often the recipients of whatever time we may have left over when everything else is done.

I maintain that the concept of "done" is not valid. When you consider you are "done," you have probably only reached a stopping point or a temporary break in the action. Are you ever really done learning, managing, mowing the lawn, or brushing your teeth? Therefore, waiting until you are "done" to activate your priority, family, or recreational time is an illogical and detrimental concept. These things should be budgeted into your time bank just like work, household chores, and everything else we must do in order to maintain our lifestyles.

For the past seven years, my Winners' Wisdom columns have been sent out to magazines, newspapers, and online publications around the world every Thursday morning without fail.

They generally take me about 10 to 15 minutes to write each week. In the past several years, I have discovered the wisdom of writing them when I have the inspiration in my mind for the week's effort. Oftentimes when I write the columns early, something time-sensitive pops up on Thursday morning, and I'm glad the column is out of the way so I am not forced to rush out something that is less than my best effort. I call this concept of moving things forward in an attempt to control my calendar "banking time."

Next time you are near a reservoir where a river has been dammed up to create a lake, observe that all the water is still there. It has simply been stored up to use at a later time for irrigation, power generation, flood control, or recreation. The water must be stored when it is available so it can be released when it is needed. Your time and the demands that are placed on your time are like that river. Either you control it, or it will control you. I am pleased to report that as I close this column it is 2:34 on Tuesday afternoon.

As you go through your day today, remember you can't control your time, but you can manage yourself.

Today's the day!

BECOMING A TORTOISE

WE ARE ALL FAMILIAR WITH THE STORY AND THE MESSAGE OF the tortoise and the hare. In this story, we learn how, even though the hare is much quicker and faster, the tortoise eventually wins the race and gets the prize.

Success in our personal and professional lives is not a matter of how well we can perform for an hour, a day, or a week; but, instead, how well we can perform over the long haul. This is true in investing. Recent statistics tell us that individual investors who try to time the market, or jump in and jump out quickly for the big profit, average 3.9 percent return over their years in the market. On the other hand, people who employ a dollar cost average technique or simply invest the same amount, at the same time each month, year after year, average 11.8 percent return.

There is nothing particularly exciting about this other than it works and can insure your long-term financial success. I like excitement in my sporting events, books, and movies. I like my life to be boring when it comes to investing, airplane rides, and business planning. Many people thrive on the excitement of getting as close to the edge as they can. I thrive on the excitement of winning as big as possible while staying as far as I can away from the dangerous edge. Consistent performance over the long haul is the key to any success.

The great actor Spencer Tracy once said that the key to a great performance is, "Show up on time, hit your mark, and know your lines."

Several college friends and I started a scholarship fund. Recently, we received some correspondence that alerted us we were coming up on our 20th anniversary of the scholarship fund. We were amazed that we have been successfully functioning for 20 years. The scholarship fund has grown and has helped many deserving students complete their education. Our founding board members of the scholarship are shocked to know how much we have done by simply starting small and staying consistent.

One of my favorite American authors, Louis L'Amour, said of one of his characters, "Nothing can stop a person who has made up his mind and will simply keep coming."

As you go through your day today, look for consistency and persistence that will make the difference in the years to come.

Today's the day!

TALKING, LISTENING, AND COMMUNICATING

RECENTLY, I HAVE BEEN DEVOTING CONSIDERABLE TIME TO studying the topic of communication and how we communicate. I became intrigued with the inner workings of communication when I heard Dr. Ray Hull, a noted expert on the topic, presenting at a U.S. Department of Education event in Washington, DC. The interest Ray created in me has grown and will culminate in a book I am coauthoring with Dr. Ray Hull entitled *The Art of Communication.*

In the course of my study, I ran across an account of a psychological experiment. In this experiment, a man was seated at a table by himself in a busy Starbucks coffee shop. On the man's table, a sign was placed that read, "Free coffee if you'll listen to my story." The man sat there patiently for several hours, but no one accepted his offer of free coffee in exchange for listening to his story.

Then a second experiment was conducted using the same man at the same table at the same Starbucks. The only variation was the sign that was changed to read, "Free coffee if you will tell me your story." A line formed at the man's table and continued to grow until the experiment had to be called off because there were too many people waiting to tell their story.

My late, great friend and colleague, Dr. Stephen Covey, was fond of saying, "Seek first to understand and then to be understood." I've long believed in the adage that people don't care how much you know until they know how much you care.

Listening to someone else is a supreme compliment and honor. We value others as we listen to their thoughts and ideas. This sets the stage for us to effectively share our own thoughts and ideas.

As a platform speaker, I regularly have the privilege of sharing the stage with many learned and luminary figures. I would like to think that success as a speaker comes from what we say or how well we say it; but in reality, the highest-paid speakers are compensated not for their message or their eloquence but for who they are.

When we meet someone we don't know, our statements to them carry little weight or impact; but if we will just listen to them, we will create trust and the beginnings of friendship. Then our words begin to matter—not as much for what we say or how we say it but for who we are.

As you go through your day today, remember to talk better as you begin by listening.

Today's the day!

THE MATURITY MATRIX

MATURITY IS A VALUABLE ASSET THAT WE ALL EVENTUALLY PAY for whether we use it or not. Maturity is applied wisdom that generally comes to us through mistakes we have made. As we get more maturity in our lives, we realize that we can actually learn from other people's mistakes. We need not experience all the pain to receive the gain.

Before we have the benefit of maturity, we too often act without thinking, getting advice, or drawing upon our life experience. Maturity allows us to pause, ponder, and then react to the world around us. We can visualize immaturity as a thermometer. It simply acts upon the environment around it. The thermometer will go up and down based on the prevailing climate without making any impact or improvement. On the other hand, a thermostat registers the temperature much like a thermometer, but it reacts to the environment so that it can control the climate instead of having the climate control it.

The modern digital age has made it possible for us to draw on the wisdom and experience of people around the world. Here in the 21ˢᵗ century, we don't need to go into any situation without learning from people who have been there before us;

however, we can learn from others' experiences without necessarily drawing the same conclusion as they did.

I'm reminded of the two 19th century shoe salesmen who were sent to remote islands in the South Pacific to sell shoes to the natives there. After several weeks traveling on a steamship, they both reached their island destination and began exploring the marketplace. After several weeks, one of the salesmen dejectedly wired a message back to the home office of the shoe manufacturer saying, "Please forward return ticket for the ship back home as these natives do not wear shoes; therefore, there is no opportunity here." The second shoe salesman experienced the same environment and conditions but drew a different conclusion. His wire read, "Please forward all available shoe inventory on the next ship. These natives do not have any shoes, and this is an unlimited opportunity here."

Applied wisdom can create opportunities, not by looking at different things but by looking at things differently. How many times have we found ourselves learning about someone else's breakthrough idea and said, "Why didn't I think of that?"

The next time you're confronted with a set of facts or someone else's experience, just ask yourself, "What am I going to wish later that I had thought of right now?"

As you go through your day today, master maturity, but react in new ways.

Today's the day!

WHAT'S ON?

ONE OF THE GREATEST INFLUENCES OF THE 20TH AND NOW THE 21st century has got to be the television. It is difficult for all but the most senior of us to imagine what life was like before that magic box came into our homes. The most magnificent, inspiring, horrific, educational, and historic images have come from all around the world and been presented to us in our living rooms.

People of our generation are connected in a way no other people throughout recorded history have ever known. We share the awareness of common sights and sounds. People everywhere know who got voted off the island or which star dances better than the other. Television makes a wonderful tool but a horrible master. Young people today spend far more time in front of a television than they do talking to their parents, studying, or engaging in exercise through playing with their peers.

One of my core professional pursuits is Narrative Television Network. NTN makes movies and television accessible for our nation's 13 million blind and visually impaired people and their families, along with millions more around the world. All of us involved with Narrative Television Network are very proud of the work we do, as television has become the greatest source of information, education, and entertainment in our society. We have become a common culture, greatly due to the impact of television.

The challenge arises when we fail to control television and allow television to control us. Unfortunately, too many people come home after work or school and simply flop down in front of the TV. If you ask them the next day what they did the previous evening, they will say, "I watched TV." However, if you ask them what they watched, they probably don't even know, or they channel surfed, catching parts of a number of programs.

With the ability to digitally record any program at any time and enjoy it at your own discretion as it fits into your schedule, there is no excuse for not making the television your slave instead of allowing it to be your master. There are any number of easily accessible program guides that allow anyone to select programs worthy of the investment of their time. Television will bring you enjoyment, education, and information, or—if it is not controlled—it can waste all of the time you have and even more.

As you go through your day today, commit to using television as the priceless tool it is instead of allowing it to be a boredom reliever or babysitter. The best that the world has to offer is as close as your TV.

Today's the day!

EFFICIENCY AND EFFECTIVENESS

MY LATE MENTOR, COLLEAGUE, AND FRIEND ZIG ZIGLAR often said, "Efficiency is doing things right. Effectiveness is doing the right things." These two terms are often used interchangeably, but they are, at their core, quite different.

Too many people in our world today are moving at warp speed in the wrong direction or without any direction at all. They may be very efficient but totally ineffective.

Effectiveness is the combination of doing the right thing at the right time for the right reason to get you from where you are to where you want to be. If you are effective, you will always be efficient; but just because you are efficient does not necessarily mean you are effective.

Only you can define your personal definition of effectiveness, because it will inevitably incorporate your life goals and the subsequent short-term goals required to get you to your destination. Others can judge your efficiency, but only you can judge your effectiveness in light of where you know you should be.

There are times in life when you don't have enough information to make a critical decision. In this case, the most effective thing you can do is sit and wait. Sitting around and apparently doing nothing does not seem efficient, but it will prove to be so in the long run if it helps you to avoid doing a U-turn and starting over. I remember my grandfather asking me, "If you don't have time to do it right, when are you going to have time to do it over?"

Sometimes it is more efficient and, therefore, more effective to take a more deliberate and measured approach to the task at hand.

One of the true gifts that came into my life was a growing friendship with legendary basketball coach John Wooden. At age 97, he remained one of the sharpest and most effective thinkers I knew. He had a tremendous capacity for cutting through the noise and clutter to get to the fundamental issue at hand.

Coach Wooden often told his players to be quick but don't hurry. Being quick means being prepared, being sharp, being aggressive. Hurrying often means being out of control, being rushed, and not being at your best. If you are going to be effective, you will always be quick, but you will never be rushed or hurried.

As you go through your day today, concentrate on being effective, and you will find that being efficient will take care of itself.

Today's the day!

PROMPT, POLITE, AND PROFESSIONAL

TIME IS THE ONLY IRREPLACEABLE—THEREFORE PRICELESS—commodity in the world. In our modern personal and professional lives, we all feel as if we are suffering from a distinct lack of time. We have as much time as anyone has ever had or will ever have. There are 24 hours each day. No one gets any more or less. In reality, you cannot waste time or save time. You can only spend it wisely or foolishly.

In our society, we expect people to respect our space, our money, our position, and any number of factors that relate to who we are; but too often, we do not expect people to respect our time. People who are habitually late for calls, appointments, or social engagements are stealing our time. These people make a habit of wandering in 10, 15, or 20 minutes late. Sometimes even later.

You have heard it said that time is money. This is true, because all of us exchange our time, effort, and energy for money and spend our money for other people's time, effort, and energy in the form of products and services; therefore, when people are late, they not only steal our time, they—in effect—steal our money. In our society, you can go to jail for stealing money but, unfortunately, when people steal your time, you often don't even get a decent apology.

I am certainly not talking about the occasional emergency that can be forgiven when someone is late. If you are on time for ten appointments in a row, an excuse of a flat tire, sick child, or other calamity is very acceptable; however, if you have been late eight out of ten times, no reason for your tardiness will suffice. It's just another in a long line of never-ending excuses.

If you want to show people that you care about them, respect them, and appreciate them, be on time. Your promptness says, "I value you, both personally and professionally. I consider our time together very important, and I have taken time out of my day to spend it with you just as you have committed your time to me."

Your lateness says, "I don't care about you. I was doing more important things before this appointment that I did not wish to interrupt for you. I did not care enough to plan my day or my travel to be here on time so that I could take advantage of every minute of the commitment you have made to me."

As you go through your day today, make a commitment to honor other people's time, and make certain they honor yours.

Today's the day!

TRAVEL TRAUMA

AS AN AUTHOR, PROFESSIONAL SPEAKER, AND PRESIDENT OF the Narrative Television Network, several times each month I find myself traveling across the country. If anyone ever tells you that traveling is glamorous, you can rest assured they haven't done much. Whether it's for business or pleasure, all of us find ourselves heading to the airport more and more often. Especially since the tragedy of September 11, air travel has become more time-consuming, crowded, and difficult.

Before you contemplate your next trip, there are several survival tips you should keep in mind.

1. *Do you really need to make this trip?* With the advent of new technology in conference calls, video conferencing, and tele-seminars, you may be able to accomplish your mission without leaving home.

2. *Direct flights are gold.* There are 22 cities throughout North America I can travel to without making a connection. You should know the direct flight destinations from your local airport, and you should update the list regularly as flights often change.

3. *The nearest airport is not always the best.* Particularly if you are flying to the East Coast or West Coast there are often two or three airports that can reasonably serve any location. Be sure to check each of these for direct flights, convenient times, etc., before you book your travel.

4. *Upgrades are heaven.* If you don't think it's worth it to fly first class, you probably haven't tried it. Most airlines offer easy frequent flyer upgrades that you should be utilizing.

5. *Get to the airport early.* You do not get bonus points for sprinting down the concourse and diving onto the plane just before they close the door. That relaxed cup of coffee or sandwich at the airport before boarding can make it a nice relaxed trip.

6. *Carry on the necessities.* If you travel enough, sooner or later you will be on one airplane and your checked luggage will be on another. Have the bare necessities of wardrobe, personal items, and material for your meeting with you at all times.

7. *Status matters.* Being a member of an airline's airport club, frequent flyer program, or bonus system can make all the difference. The Admiral's Club and other airlines private clubs are great places to relax, work, or have a meeting.

8. *Maximize your travel time.* Time on flights and waiting for flights are perfect for computer work, reading, or listening to audio books. Don't waste this time.

9. *Combine trips whenever possible.* If you're going to have to be in LA, DC, or New York for a couple of days, go through your Rolodex to determine what other contacts you can make or meetings you can have to maximize the time and expense of the trip.

10. *Patience is a virtue.* Stay calm, be flexible, and always have at least one backup flight. Remember, if you take the first flight of the day, you are statistically far more likely to arrive on time with your luggage in your hand.

As you go through your day today, consider the investment of time, effort, and money you make in travel, and make your travel work for you.

Today's the day!

INTEGRITY

LOADED GUN

DURING THE FRONTIER TIMES AS AMERICA WAS EXPANDING, most people carried a loaded gun. The vast majority of these people treated their loaded gun with respect and used it with wisdom. Here in the 21ˢᵗ century, few of us carry a loaded gun on a daily basis, but we all have ready access to something that can be just as dangerous if not handled properly.

In the blink of an eye, each of us can whip out an ink pen and sign our name. This seemingly insignificant act can commit you for a lifetime and beyond to numerous things whether you understand them or not. Many legal and financial problems are caused by something as simple as signing your name to a document you didn't thoroughly read or understand.

There are few activities in your personal and professional life that create an absolute among all of us. This column is read by several million people each week, reading hundreds of magazine, newspaper, or online publications. If anyone disagrees with the following statement, please use the contact information at the end of this book to let me know. But until I hear otherwise, it goes unchallenged that you should never sign your name to anything you don't fully understand and agree with. It doesn't matter what was said or what you assumed or what was advertised. What matters in a contract-driven litigious world is what you signed.

If you are entering into a transaction such as a real estate purchase or a will and estate matter, it is another absolute rule that you must have an attorney or other qualified representative there who is looking out for your interests only. Never let anyone represent both you and another party in a complex transaction. Even if you're buying a house and signing numerous voluminous documents that you don't have the ability or willingness to digest, you must have a competent representative who has explained everything to your satisfaction.

Use your signature as if it were a loaded gun that could hurt or even kill you. In a business and financial sense, it is just that.

As you go through your day today, remember that your signature is a powerful and precious tool.

Today's the day!

AN OASIS IN THE INSANITY

MY LATE, GREAT FRIEND AND MENTOR PAUL HARVEY DELIV-
ered the news faithfully to several generations of Americans.
Beyond his regular newscasts, Mr. Harvey became known for
a regular feature he called "The Rest of the Story." Since you've
probably just been exposed to the doom and gloom, disasters,
controversy, and turmoil that make up the news, I thought I
might reach back and borrow some wit and wisdom from Paul
Harvey as I deliver my own "rest of the story" as a counterpoint to the news of the day.

I'm well aware that readers around the world will receive
this story through many sources, so it may be delivered to
them any time throughout a three- or four-week period, but I
am confident my own counterpoint to the news will be up-to-
the-minute, timely, and relevant whether you read it next week,
next month, or next year.

Today, there were millions of dedicated people who got
up, took care of their families, went to work, created value for
their employers and customers, and made the world a better
place. Their children went to school, studied diligently, and

learned their lessons, which will become the basis for the innovation and developments that will improve lives throughout this century.

In other news, countless politicians, public officials, business and community leaders acted honorably and performed well in the face of the ongoing temptation to lie, cheat, and steal. It was reported that many thousands of passionate entrepreneurs demonstrated their ongoing belief in the American dream and launched a variety of businesses and ventures that will create jobs and fuel our economy through the coming decades.

Over the weekend, it was reported that millions of families gathered privately or collectively in their houses of worship to give thanks for all that they have and focus on the principles that will lead and guide them toward a better tomorrow. In sports, many aspiring athletes trained hard, dedicated themselves, and focused on their goals. Some of them succeeded while others stumbled and fell, but most got up, dusted themselves off, and will be trying harder next season.

On the weather front, there were the inevitable natural disasters causing much damage, many injuries, and some loss of human lives; however, in related stories, neighbors rescued neighbors, public servants and first responders performed heroically, and it is anticipated that things will get back to normal in the coming days. There were countless reports of outbreaks of random acts of human kindness across the country and around the world. Reports came in indicating people opened doors for one another, allowed other motorists to go first in traffic, and offered millions of winks, nods, and kind words at just the right times and in just the right places.

In conclusion, as we wrap up the news of today and tomorrow, the good guys won, best efforts were rewarded, kindness was reciprocated, global problems were solved as others appeared on the horizon awaiting solutions in the future, and it's a great day today; but we are assured that tomorrow can be even better.

As you go through your day today, follow the news but don't forget the rest of the story.

Today's the day!

BALANCING THE SCALES

COMPLAINTS HAVE BECOME AN EPIDEMIC IN OUR WORLD TODAY. Complaining is the latest and most popular full-contact sport in our society. Unfortunately, when you constantly and aggressively complain about poor performance and bad service, your verbal assaults and admonishments often fall on deaf ears. This is a result of the scales being out of balance. Your complaints are piled on top of everyone else's complaints, creating a constant stream of complaint-filled conversation.

The people with hotels, restaurants, airlines, and all manner of businesses that hear these complaints are not able to distinguish them from all the other noise around them, because this is all they ever hear. Too often, we feel pre-programmed to catch people doing something wrong and tell them all about it.

I am on an ongoing quest to catch people doing something right and let them know about it. This makes me feel better. It makes them feel better. And I have been surprised to learn that it actually makes my complaints, suggestions, and constructive criticism more valid when a difficult situation arises.

When you find someone doing a menial, clerical, or service job well, be sure to tell them. Yours may be the only compliment they have received in weeks or even months. You will make their day, and I assure you that you will feel better. The serendipity will come into play when you find that if you require anything extra or have a situation you need corrected, these people will go out of their way to promptly and professionally serve you.

Recently, I had a flight attendant greet me by name as I walked onto a jet. Immediately my ego kicked in, and I assumed she recognized me from television, one of my convention or arena speeches, or possibly one of my brief appearances in a movie. It turns out it was nothing quite that grandiose.

When I inquired how she knew my name, she informed me that I had been on a flight of hers several weeks previously, and I had complimented her on the meal and on the service. I will admit to you that I do not even remember the occasion that she referred to as it has become my practice to catch people doing something right. I did find it fascinating that, out of the thousands of passengers she encountered throughout a month, she remembered me simply from a brief compliment.

As you go through your day today, if you want to stand out from the crowd, don't complain the loudest. Just catch people doing something right.

Today's the day!

DOING YOUR BEST

THE LITTLE THINGS

WE ARE ALL RUSHED AND CRUNCHED FOR TIME IN OUR WORLD today; therefore, anything you choose to do should be done with your best effort or not at all. With so many responsibilities and opportunities before each of us daily, there is no time nor reason to be mediocre at anything.

Everyone understands the urgency of performing well in the tasks they consider to be "big things," but they too often overlook matters they consider to be "little things." If you really analyze the areas of your life, either personally or professionally, that you consider to be "big things," you will find, if you look closely enough, that they are nothing more than a series or group of "little things."

You may run the best, most efficient business operation ever known to humankind, but if your people don't answer the phone politely and professionally, or if they don't invest the time and energy to simply get people's names right, you are wasting your time.

Our most precious possession is our name. One of the elements that distinguishes world class service from standard service—whether it be business, dining, hotel, transportation, etc.—is that the world class professionals greet you politely, energetically, and use your name correctly.

There is a certain group of business "experts" who believe that in order to be successful we must practice intimidation. While I disagree with this philosophy, there is an amazing learning opportunity for us all within these intimidation theories. These adversarial intimidators would tell you that the best way to "put someone down" or try to establish your own superiority is simply to mispronounce or misuse their name.

The most amazing, thoughtful, meaningful, and significant message can be diminished by a simple typographical error. No matter how profound the words on the page may be, if they contain sloppy errors, you may as well stamp the words in bright red across the top of the page: "I really don't care very much about this."

You've heard it said countless times, but it is as true today as the first time you heard it. People don't care how much you know until they know how much you care. If you want to show people how much you care, pay attention to the little things, and you will find the big things take care of themselves.

As you go through your day today, do everything as if it alone will make the difference between success and failure. You will find that it does.

Today's the day!

THE MYTH OF CONTROL

ALL OF US WANT TO CONTROL OUR ENVIRONMENT, OUR CIR-
cumstances, our lifestyle, and our future.

Control is an illusion. Ask the people in New Orleans
who went through Hurricane Katrina.

You can plan, prepare, insure, and insulate, but when it's
all said and done, there are times that, in spite of all of our
best efforts, bad things happen to good people.

Mark Twain said, "Climate is what we all want. Weather
is what we all live with." I am an eternal optimist. I believe
in, and expect, the very best in every situation; however, I
understand that there are only three things I can control in
life that affect everything I will ever do, know, have, and
experience. All we can control are our choices, our attitude,
and our effort.

1. *Choices.* We are all the beneficiary or the victim of the
choices we have made in the past. Everything we have in our
personal and professional lives, at this point, is a result of our
prior choices. Only when we accept this responsibility can we
live today and every day in the certain knowledge that our
future will be what we want it to be based on the choices we

make today. We don't always choose what happens to us in life, but we can always choose what we're going to do about it. For every person devastated by Katrina, I can show you someone who is overcoming and actually moving ahead in the aftermath of the disaster.

2. *Attitude.* Nothing can impact how we live and succeed more than our attitude. Abraham Lincoln said, "People are about as happy as they decide to be." One of the exercises from my book *The Ultimate Gift* that I encourage people to pursue is called The Golden List. The Golden List is simply the practice of regularly listing things for which you are thankful. A few moments a day engaging in creating a Golden List will ensure you have a great attitude. Having a great attitude will ensure you have a great day and a great life.

3. *Effort.* In all of the success manuals, speeches, how-to books, and success courses, the most overlooked element in the arena of achievement, happiness, and fulfillment is a simple little four-letter word. "Work" is the key to all of your goals and dreams. If I knew of a shortcut, I would have already taken it, and I would be pleased to tell you about it. It doesn't exist. I have had the privilege of working with some of the greatest people of the 20th and 21st centuries on stage, on television, in movies, and in the context of my books. When you get past all of the money, power, prestige, and fame, you are left with one overwhelming impression— all successful people have put forth an amazing effort.

As you go through your day today, cease worrying and concern about things you cannot control, and focus on the things you can.

Today's the day!

THE PUNCTUALITY PLEDGE

IN THE MODERN WORLD, WE SPEND A LOT OF TIME, EFFORT, energy, and money to try and let people know that we care about them. Whether it's a thank you note, flowers, a greeting card, or simply a quick email, the personal touch is always appropriate and always appreciated; however, it's important to remember that these tangible symbols can never take the place of our day-to-day actions.

As you interact daily with others, there are two things that they value highly. People treasure their name and their time. If you want to show disrespect to someone, simply forget their name or say it improperly. For thousands of years across many cultures, one of the great insults has always been to disregard remembering or pronouncing properly someone's name.

The second treasure you must respect beyond people's name is their time. When you can't remember their name, you are saying, "I don't care about you." When you are habitually late, you are saying, "My time is more important than your time," or "I am more important than you."

No amount of flowers or greeting cards will ever overcome treading on people's treasures. Your actions and your gestures speak louder than your words.

In the corporate world, there has been a recent proliferation of scheduled phone calls. This is to say, instead of simply calling someone and discussing the matter at hand, it has become trendy to have your assistant call and set up a scheduled phone conference for some point in the future.

Certainly if you have a number of details to discuss that will take a prolonged period, scheduling a block of time for an appropriate conversation may be valid. But more and more often, people are having their assistants set up calls for them and even place the call so that the other person is on the line first.

Unless you're the pope or the president of the United States, it's probably best to dial the phone yourself and ask to speak to the person you want to speak to. But, in any case, if you're going to set up a pre-scheduled telephone conference, by all means be on time. Otherwise, when you have your assistant set up the call, you are communicating, "My time is so valuable that I can't waste a minute." But at the appointed hour for the call, if you're not on the line, you're further communicating, "Your time doesn't matter to me at all." Certainly always speak to people whenever possible with polite, professional respect; but remember, no matter what you say, your actions speak more loudly.

As you go through your day today, look for ways to not only be efficient, but also to politely and professionally communicate appropriate messages through your actions.

Today's the day!

DEFINITIONS AND LIMITATIONS

MOST PROJECTS GO THROUGH TWO PHASES: CREATION AND production. In some cases this might be called ideas and follow through. These are two totally separate and distinct functions. Both functions are imperative, but they are far from interchangeable and should not be intermingled if you are going to be maximizing your potential.

My late, great friend Robert Schuller often said, "Never get the 'how are you going to do it' phase mixed up in the 'what are you going to do' phase." What this means is that we should never limit what we are going to do based on the things we know how to do.

If you decide to travel from your hometown to a distant city, there are a myriad of variables that can impact your trip that cannot be anticipated. You simply can't wait until all the traffic lights are green before you leave home. Your flight may be delayed, there may be detours along the highway, or you can experience car trouble and other unforeseen challenges.

In order for you to arrive at your destination, you must first establish your destination and then begin your journey. While planning is important, some of the variables must be dealt with while you're on the move.

In my organization, there are idea people and there are logistical people. They are both valuable within their own time and place; however, if you get the logistical people involved while you're in the idea stage, they will begin anticipating problems and formulating contingencies for things you are only considering. This will limit your ideas and the scope of your potential greatly.

On the other hand, if you simply turn the idea people loose, they will come up with endless big-picture thoughts that may not be practical or even doable. You really need a two-phased approach. First, you decide what you are going to do, considering elements such as: Is it good? Is it right? Is it beneficial? Is it profitable? And does it line up with our mission? Then you move to the second phase and deal with questions such as: What will it cost? How will it impact what we are doing now? What are all of the anticipated challenges? How will we deal with unforeseen contingencies? And many others.

I have met many would-be authors who have a title in mind, and they are trying to write a book to fit their title. Labels are important once you establish a product or service, but be careful not to limit something by virtue of its definition or title.

As you go through your day today, imagine the possibilities, then consider the practicalities.

Today's the day!

KEEPING SCORE

IN OUR HECTIC, FAST-PACED WORLD TODAY, WHEN IT'S ALL SAID and done, there is an awful lot said and very little done. People talk a good game but rarely do they get around to playing it. We all have more information, knowledge, and expertise than it would take for several people to succeed.

Unfortunately, we don't succeed for knowing something or learning something. We succeed from *doing* something. It is far better to apply one principle in the real world than to learn ten principles that remain abstract theories to us.

There are three states of existence that matter in this discussion: being, doing, and having. In our commercialized world today, everyone wants to have everything now. They don't want to do anything to get it or be the kind of person who can have it, they simply want to be given everything instantly. The universe is set up so that if you will *be* the kind of person who will then *do* the right thing, you can eventually *have* everything you want.

Like any other equation, when we get the elements out of order, we are headed for disaster. When you want to have things today and pay for them tomorrow, or receive compensation now for effort you will expend later, you are traveling on an unsustainable path.

Each generation of parents wants their children to live better than they do. This is good and admirable. Parents have felt this way since the beginning of recorded history; however, our commercialized, instant information society has made this generation's young people not only want to exceed their parents' standard of living, but do it now if not yesterday.

You never do anything good or bad that you don't get paid for. You have heard it said a thousand times that you reap what you sow. Too many people are trying to sow one thing and reap something else—or worse yet, sow nothing and enjoy a huge harvest today. Nothing is as easy, simple, or fast as we would like it to be, but the fruits of our labor are, indeed, sweet, life sustaining, and more than a fair exchange for our toil.

The next time you are communicating with a parent, teacher, or mentor about the success they have achieved or the level of accomplishment they have obtained, don't just dwell on the finish line they have crossed, but learn all you can about the journey they have traveled and the race they have run.

As you go through your day today, focus not on what you have or even what you want to do, but who you want to be.

Today's the day!

LOOKING FOR WORK

RECENT ECONOMIC CONDITIONS HAVE CREATED AN ENVIRON-
ment in which many people have been laid off and are currently
looking for work. A recent book by a good friend of mine
recounted stories from dozens of famous and successful people who, at one point, were laid off or fired; but they now look
back on that time and realize it was a great turning point in
their lives.

When you're looking for work, there are several things you
should keep in mind. There are jobs, and there are vocations.
Both can be appropriate at various points in time. When you
are young, learning a profession, or suddenly out of work and
need income, you should take a job. A job may consist of
any legal, moral, and honorable work that will bring you the
income you need to stay alive until you can find your vocation.

A vocation is the work you do because you love it, it makes
a difference in the world, and fulfills your own destiny. If you
pursue your vocation, you will never work a day in your life,
or at least you won't feel like you work a day in your life.

One of the biggest problems in our society today is the
growing number of people who are diligently looking for

work right up until the time they get a job, and then they quit looking for work. This is to say that there are a lot of people who, unfortunately, do not know the satisfaction, pride, and dignity that comes from doing an honest day's work on their job that provides service and value in the lives of others.

At my company, Narrative Television Network, we have offices and studio facilities spread out over two different floors in a commercial office building. For a number of years, we have had difficulties with the people cleaning our building. The difficulty was that they, quite simply, didn't clean the building. Finally, we were assigned a new professional to clean our offices and studios. A young lady named Kristle began cleaning for us recently, and it has been a wonderful experience for all of us. The amazing thing about her performance is she politely, professionally, and thoroughly cleans our building.

Unfortunately, this has become a far-too-rare occurrence when you hire people in our society today. Think back over the products and services you have purchased with your hard-earned dollars over the past several months. How often do you not get what you were promised? How often do you have to have people come back multiple times to do a single job? How often do you have to put up with attitudes that well-served customers should not experience?

As sad as this is in the marketplace today, it represents an opportunity for you and me; because just like Kristle, if you will do your job on time every time, politely and professionally, with a good attitude, you will stand out from your competition, and you can't help but succeed.

As you go through your day today, do your work as if it mattered, because it does.

Today's the day!

LOOK FOR OPPORTUNITIES

OBSERVATIONS ON OPPORTUNITY

RECENTLY I ATTENDED MY 30-YEAR HIGH SCHOOL REUNION. AS a blind person, I sat and listened to the conversations and observations of those around me. The most common comment was, "I'm surprised they turned out like that." Apparently, everyone turned out either better or worse, but certainly different from what was expected.

As young people, we do not come with a label that says "Future Brain Surgeon" or "Soon-to-be-Unemployed Alcoholic." Opportunity is much the same. You've heard frustrated investors lament, "If I'd only bought Microsoft back then." Well, unfortunately, Microsoft didn't look like Microsoft back then.

Opportunities and possibilities more often come packaged as problems and challenges. The only thing you must do to have a great idea is to go through your daily routine and wait for something bad to happen. When it does, ask the magic question, "How could I have avoided that?" The answer to that question will be a great idea. The only thing you need to do to have a great business opportunity is to ask yourself, "How could I help other people avoid their problems?"

The answer to that question can make you rich, famous, and successful in every way.

If you read biographies of great inventors, initially you're struck by the fact that their ideas and innovations made total sense. They seem so obvious now in retrospect. When you think of living in the horse-and-buggy days when Orville and Wilbur Wright are building a plane, it seems to be a logical fit and an exciting opportunity. If you're struggling by candlelight when Thomas Edison invents a light bulb, it seems revolutionary and readily apparent. If you're waiting weeks or even months for correspondence when Alexander Graham Bell invents the telephone, it seems transformational; however, if you will read in depth the biographies of these innovators and many others, you will find that, quite often, their greatest struggles were not developing a new invention, but instead, their greatest struggles were often convincing bankers, investors, and business leaders of the validity of their inventions.

Remember, opportunities never appear in nice, clean, wrapped packages with neon signs that say OPPORTUNITY. You've got to dig a little.

As you go through your day today, look for opportunities disguised as problems.

Today's the day!

When Lightning Strikes

IT WAS AN ORDINARY DAY IN 1999. I WENT TO MY OFFICE, WENT about my daily tasks, and all seemed right—or at least normal—in the world. One of the tasks on my calendar involved writing a book and getting the manuscript off to the publisher. I had written six books previously, but they had all been nonfiction. As those six volumes had taken up most everything I knew and lots of things I merely suspected, it was time to take a different approach on book number seven.

I sat down to begin dictating a novel. Since I had no knowledge or experience in writing novels, there wasn't much cluttering up my mind. The only advice I gave myself was the advice I had heard as far back as I could remember growing up as a child in my parents' home. "Whatever you decide to do, do your best." This is important advice, and it's easy to miss the critical point.

Obviously, you want to do your best. Where a lot of us fall down is in deciding to do the right thing.

I have spoken in arenas for years to many thousands of sales people and business leaders. They deal with countless people each day. Many of those encounters are not important, while a few of them are critical; and every once in a while, the lightning will strike. Unfortunately, you and I never know when the lightning is going to strike, so all we can do is our best at everything we decide to do.

You never know when a chance meeting is going to turn into a million dollar opportunity or a lifelong personal transformation. You never know when that single call, letter, or email is going to be the one that makes the connection of your life. And—for those of us who from time to time through art, music, the spoken word, or our writing get to briefly be creative—it's simply impossible to tell when the lightning is going to strike and the whole world will change.

That first novel I sat down to do my best on in 1999 was written in five short days and published just as I dictated it, word for word. *The Ultimate Gift* has become a worldwide phenomenon selling over 3 million books and was released as a major motion picture starring James Garner, Lee Meriwether, and Brian Dennehy.

Think of the times in your life when the lightning struck and you and those around you were forever changed. If you will but focus on the possibilities, you will never do anything less than your very best.

As you go through your day today, do the best you can at everything you decide to do, and trust that the lightning will strike when and where it is supposed to.

Today's the day!

THE FOUR MINUTE
TRANSFORMATION

IN LESS THAN FOUR MINUTES FROM NOW, YOU WILL HAVE COM-
pleted reading this column. Four minutes seems like an
insignificant amount of time, and—in many endeavors of
life—it is. There was a time when breaking the four-minute
mile was the most controversial topic in the field of sports and
human endeavor. For many decades, people had approached
running a mile in four minutes, but no one had ever run a mile
in less than four minutes.

Many coaches, commentators, and even physicians felt that
it was impossible. There were dire warnings of permanent heart
and lung damage or even death resulting from running so fast
over such a long distance. Then one day, in one particular race,
Roger Bannister ran just a few seconds faster than anyone had
done before. He created the four minute transformation that, if
understood, will not only apply to runners but to your performance level in every area of your life.

Although there had been literally thousands of world class
runners around the globe trying to break this record, it had
never been done; however, the week after Roger Bannister
broke the barrier, there were five runners who equaled the feat.

Within a year of Bannister's sub-four minute mile, 54 runners around the world had done it. A few years later, high school competitors were routinely breaking the four minute mile.

It would be impossible to convince any thinking person that the state of training and competition was such that 54 people broke the same record the same year. Instead, we have to recognize that there was a mental and emotional component to this phenomenon. People couldn't break the record because "No one had done it before." Once someone had done it, it entered the realm of possibility. This releases creativity and power that results in performance.

There are high level performers who can do anything if they can see that it is possible. There are high-level pioneers like Roger Bannister who break the barrier and set the standard for others to follow.

As you go through your day today, think of all the things that you do simply because "That's the way we always do it." Conversely, think of all the things you don't do, or even attempt, because "No one's ever done it that way before." Remember, what someone else has or has not done will not affect you if you are a performance pioneer.

Today's the day!

WHAT IF?

RECENTLY, I HEARD A RADIO PROMOTION ABOUT A CASINO that was offering senior citizens free chips that they could bring to the casino and gamble with. The tag line of the radio ad asked a poignant question, "What have you got to lose?" Obviously, in the casino context, they are implying that you have nothing to lose, and this may be true if you don't consider your time and the percentage of people on whom the casino is banking will lose their free chips and gamble much more.

The point here is the compelling question: "What do you have to lose?" We spend a great deal of time, effort, energy, and money managing risk in our lives. Risk is perceived by the masses to be avoiding bad things that can happen if they engage in certain activities or pursue certain objectives.

Whether you invest money, cross the street, start a business, attempt to begin a relationship, or stay at home and do nothing, you engage in certain risks. There is no risk-free activity. The best you and I can hope to do is weigh the risk of a certain course of action against the potential reward or possible loss.

An investment is deemed to be risky if there is a possibility of losing principle; therefore, on the surface it would appear to be risk-free if you locked away cash in a safe or strong box. In

reality, this would historically prove to be the most risky decision you could ever make, because inflation would invariably
erode your purchasing power and you would have lost your
principle, which was the very definition of risk you were trying
to avoid when you locked your money away.

Many would-be entrepreneurs face the prospect of risk.
Well-meaning friends and family members will warn of the
lack of security, failure rate in the marketplace, etc. In reality,
if you have a great idea, tremendous drive, and uncommon persistence, not pursuing your entrepreneurial dream could be the
riskiest course of action you could take. Anytime someone asks
you, "What if something bad happens?" you must consider
that, but at the same time ask yourself, "What if something
good happens?"

Change is inevitable, risk is unavoidable, and possibilities
are endless. You must find the balance between viewing life
from the mountaintop and getting too close to the cliff's edge.
As you go through your day today, welcome risk as an opportunity that you must balance.

Today's the day!

ILLUSION AND REALITY

I HAVE HAD THE PRIVILEGE OF HAVING FOUR OF MY NOVELS, TO date, turned into movies. The process of making a movie is far from the experience of enjoying a movie. Making a movie is tedious, time-consuming, and—quite simply—hard work.

In each of my movie projects, I strived to tell a great story and help people examine their own reality. There is probably less reality in the movie business than anywhere in the world except for reality television. Illusions are not reality, but they can teach us and motivate us. Given a strong enough image, an illusion will eventually become reality.

Several years ago, I had the opportunity to work with the actor Gary Busey. Gary is known for many things on and off the screen, but I believe Gary Busey's greatest accomplishment was playing Buddy Holly in *The Buddy Holly Story*. Busey not only came to life on the screen as Buddy Holly, he performed much of Buddy Holly's well-known music. When shown pictures of Buddy Holly and Gary Busey side by side, more people identify Busey as Buddy Holly than identify the real Buddy Holly.

Early in my career, I got to meet and interview the great actor Douglas Fairbanks Jr. Fairbanks is best known for his movie roles in the 1940s and 50s; but when I got to know him, I was most intrigued to learn about his boyhood years. His father, Douglas Fairbanks Sr., and his stepmother Mary Pickford, partnered with Charlie Chaplin to found one of the great movie studios *United Artists*. Douglas Fairbanks Jr. told me that growing up with Charlie Chaplin as a family friend was a great adventure for him when he was a young boy. Mr. Fairbanks described Charlie Chaplin as "the perfect playmate for an eight-year-old boy."

Chaplin was an iconic figure of his time and among the best-known actors during the silent movie era. At the height of his popularity, Chaplin heard that they were having a Charlie Chaplin look-alike contest in Times Square in New York City. Chaplin decided to get dressed in his famous movie wardrobe and enter the contest himself. Ironically, the real Charlie Chaplin took third place in a Charlie Chaplin look-alike contest. Illusions can not only impact reality, but perceptions can become reality.

If you will focus on your dreams and visions of the future, you will find that, with persistence, they will become reality.

As you go through your day today, remember today's illusion can be tomorrow's reality.

Today's the day!

Cash is Still King

ALL OF US WHO ARE IN BUSINESS SHOULD PLAY TO WIN. WE keep score using money. While I would be the first to say that significance, service, values, and making a difference for others should be primary goals in our work, each of these areas benefits from more resources.

Money doesn't equal good. It does equal more. If it is your goal to do good things and make a difference in the world, money will help you do better things and make a bigger difference. The value of any organization can be calculated in numerous ways and is often a matter of debate, but cash is universal. Everyone on the planet knows what a dollar is worth.

I heard that the Apple Corporation has more cash on hand than the United States government. This made me feel good about the money I have invested in Apple and not so good about the money I have invested, via taxes, in the United States government. Companies and people who generate and keep cash have the most value.

There was a study done revealing the overall growth and return on various classes of stock since 1927. It was revealed that if you had invested $1,000 in the stock of companies that did not pay dividends, which are generally considered growth stocks, over the ensuing 80 years, your $1,000 would have grown to in excess of $800,000. This is a tremendous return, but the study went on to reveal that the same $1,000 investment in 1927 among the one-third of publicly-traded companies that paid the lowest dividends would have grown to $1.3 million. The same investment in companies that ranked among the middle one-third of dividends paid to shareholders would have turned into $4 million; and before you invest your money, you need to know that $1,000 invested among companies that ranked in the upper one-third of dividends paid would have grown to $7.9 million.

Conventional wisdom would tell us that investing in startup companies that don't pay any dividends will yield the highest results when, in reality, investing in companies that are already successful and have enough cash on hand to pay out dividends to investors will yield 10 times more investment return.

Before you invest, it's great to study charts, graphs, trends, and industry analyses, but before you put down your hard-earned dollars, take a hint from Jerry McGuire and ask someone to "Show me the money."

As you go through your day today, observe potential, examine trends, but count the cash.

Today's the day!

A CHANGE OF MIND

SEVERAL TIMES EACH MONTH, I GET TO LEAVE MY CORPORATE world job as the president of a television network and travel to an arena or a convention center somewhere in the world to make a speech. In each of these speeches, my main theme is "You change your life when you change your mind." This seems exceedingly simple as do most profound truths.

Everything you will ever do, know, have, give, and create first begins with a thought in your mind. Every good or bad thought can create an action and a corresponding result. If you want to change any aspect of your life, you first must change your mind.

Your current situation is the result of the thoughts and attitudes as well as the knowledge you have accumulated to this point. One of my favorite quotes from several of the 12 Step programs is, "Your best thinking has gotten you to this point." This is to say that everything you know and think has brought you to this place in your life. Before you can change where you are, you must change what you think, feel, and know.

Bad thoughts and attitudes do not simply spring up, fully developed, into your mind. Instead, they are the result of emotional erosion over years and decades. In order to change these thoughts, you're going to have to work on them constantly and experience some discomfort. It is as if you wanted to develop a long-unused muscle. First, you will experience some discomfort, then some soreness, but if you persist you will find yourself in possession of powers you never had before.

I am a firm believer in free enterprise capitalism. I believe the greatest good flows to the most people when they enjoy the fruits of their own efforts; however, if simply as an experiment we divided up all of the money and resources evenly among everyone, within a few short years the money would find its way back to the wealthy and successful people who have it now.

When you understand this phenomenon, you begin to know that money is not the precious commodity. Knowledge and attitude become what we all should seek. If you begin to know things you have never known and hold attitudes that you have never experienced, the success you seek will be soon to follow.

You have heard it said that "if you keep doing the same things, you will get the same results." Furthermore, if you keep thinking and believing the same things, you will continue to do the same things that have brought you to this place.

As you go through your day today, seek opportunities to learn new things and develop new attitudes.

Today's the day!

OPPORTUNITY

THE WHOLE WORLD IS LOOKING FOR A GREAT OPPORTUNITY, and they trip over one about three times each week. Opportunity is little more than the solution to a problem. The greater the problem, the greater the opportunity. Opportunity is the process of implementing a great idea.

If you want to have a great idea, simply go through your daily routine and wait for a problem or obstacle to appear. When it does, simply ask yourself, "How could I have avoided or overcome that problem?" The answer to that question is a great idea. To convert that great idea into an opportunity, simply ask yourself, "How could I help other people avoid or overcome that same problem?" The answer to that question is a great opportunity.

Andy Rooney said, "I've learned that opportunities are never lost; someone will take the ones you miss." How many times have you seen a new product, service, or concept and thought, "Why didn't I think of that?" Or, even worse yet, come to the realization that you did think of that but failed to act upon it.

Remember, in order to have an opportunity, you have to have an idea and implementation. One without the other is meaningless. Once you grasp this concept, you will begin to look at problems as potential opportunities that need to be harvested immediately. If you're facing a problem or a challenge in your life, you must assume that a multitude of other people are dealing with the same situation. In the future, you will be providing the solution to their problem, or they will be providing the solution to your problem.

One of the best examples I have ever seen of someone who experienced a problem, overcame it, and now helps others overcome that same problem via a tremendous opportunity is my friend Harland C. Stonecipher, Founder/CEO of Pre-Paid Legal Services, Inc. Harland often says, "Out of every problem or difficulty, there is an equal or greater opportunity. We must keep that in mind and look for the opportunity. Mine was an automobile accident in 1969." Harland's accident and the ensuing legal problems spawned a solution for Harland, as well as many others, and an opportunity for countless people to achieve their goals.

Once an opportunity is implemented, it can become like fine wine in that it improves with age and increases in value. But until you implement your idea, it is like a ripe fruit that will decrease in value quickly and become worthless in the very near future.

Ideas and opportunities are not given to us as a gift. They are loaned to us as a responsibility. If we don't act upon them, someone else will fill the void. Every great success and every significant fortune came from someone recognizing a problem, creating an idea surrounding the solution, and then implementing it. Problems are normal. Ideas are commonplace. But implementation, resulting in opportunity, is the stuff dreams are made of.

As you go through your day today, welcome problems, embrace ideas, and implement solutions in the form of opportunity.

Today's the day!

CHOOSING ADVICE
WISELY

Making Choices and Decisions

When speaking at an arena event, business convention, or corporate meeting, I can count on the audience being completely silent when I tell them, "You are where you are in every area of your personal and professional life because of the choices you've made in the past. Or if I were to put that another way, all of the decisions you have made in your entire life have brought you to this place, at this time, sitting in that chair right now."

I want all of my audiences and you, my reader, to understand that only when we accept the responsibility for the choices we have made that have brought us to this point can we then accept the potential surrounding the fact that tomorrow will be anything we want it to be based upon the decisions we make today.

I cannot tell you what constitutes the right choices or decisions in your life, but I can give you three tips that can help you through the process.

1. Choose what will make you happy tomorrow. Almost all decisions come with an option that will make you feel good now as well as a choice that will make you feel good later. As

in most situations in life, delayed gratification will always lead to the destiny you seek.

2. Don't make any decisions until you have to. Good decisions come from evaluating all the facts objectively. Making a decision before you have all the facts is a sure road to failure. While you don't want to make decisions too late after some of the doors of opportunity have closed, you never want to make a decision before you have to.

3. Choose the option that will leave you more choices. When in doubt about the course of action to pursue, lean toward the one that gives you more choices and options for the future. Choices and options are a valuable commodity. If deciding on one course versus the other will keep your options open, this is always a benefit.

Seeking advice from experienced people is always a wise course of action, but never take advice from anyone who doesn't have what you want. Fat diet doctors, broke investment counselors, and incarcerated defense lawyers should be avoided. Once you have identified all your options, weighed all the information, and made the best decision you can, don't look back, and never second guess. When it comes to making good choices and proper decisions, all you can do is all you can do.

As you go through your day today, build the tomorrow you want by making good choices and right decisions now.

Today's the day!

A DISEASE CALLED MORE

YEARS OF SUCCESS AND PROSPERITY IN OUR ECONOMY HAVE created a consumer-based society. We are no longer worried about our physical or financial survival; therefore, we have undertaken a new challenge. As a people, we have embraced the elusive challenge of accumulating more. Please understand that there is absolutely nothing wrong with enjoying material possessions. It is important, however, to draw a distinction between the possessions we have and those possessions that have us.

If your goal is to acquire a certain standard of living or lifestyle for you and your family or for your future security, this is admirable. However, if it is your burning desire to keep up with the image portrayed by the commercials on television or in the glamour magazines, you have been afflicted with the dreaded disease called more, discussed briefly toward the beginning of the book.

More is a disease that feeds upon itself like a thirst that can never be quenched. As we rush about aimlessly trying to accumulate more, we become aware of even a greater number of things we don't have and must obtain. Instead of seeking the impossible goal of reaching *more,* we should, instead, seek the internal goal called *enough.*

Ironically, we can find people who are literally billionaires and who have long ago lost count of all of their possessions. However, these people are still driven on that eternal quest for more. On the other hand, there are people of seemingly modest means who have attained the admirable state of enough. They no longer judge themselves based on what they have, but instead on who they are. They have come to the conclusion that it is more important to be someone special than to have a vast accumulation of possessions. They have reached a state of being where they understand that it is not important to be a "human having." It is only important to arrive as a "human being."

In the final analysis, many times reaching the state of enough will give you the confidence and peace of mind to be an even better person who will attract more success, resulting in the tangible possessions that have become such an addiction in our society. Focus on who you are, and allow what you have to become a result of your personal success.

Today's the day!

ONE SEASON OF HOPE

AS THE AUTHOR OF MORE THAN 30 BOOKS, I HAVE COME TO anticipate that time once or twice each year when one of my books is released. *One Season of Hope* was released in April 2015 and is the first novel in my new *Homecoming Historical Series.* These books, and hopefully movies, each take place in a fictional high school named for a real historical figure. While you're reading a compelling and inspiring story going on in and around the high school, you will also be exposed to a unique historical perspective from the point of view of the high school's namesake.

Harry S. Truman High School is the setting for *One Season of Hope,* so modern-day high school students, teachers, and coaches interact with and learn from the historical life lessons offered by President Truman.

Hope is the most vital element of humanity. In his classic epic tale *The Inferno*, Dante wrote about a fictional descent beneath the earth. At the end of the journey, Dante takes his readers to the gates of Hell on which is inscribed the poignant message, "Abandon all hope here." Hope is the beginning of dreams, efforts, achievement, and success. As long as we have hope, we have possibilities. Once hope is gone, nothing can exist.

The most valuable thing you can give another person is a feeling of hope. Once you've gone through a difficult setback, illness, or challenge, you can make a lasting difference by finding others facing the same obstacles and sharing hope with them. The simple fact that you survived the seemingly-insurmountable situation they are facing is the beginning of hope.

One Season of Hope is the story of a young man facing life-and-death issues in the midst of what should be the most carefree, joyous time of life. I am looking forward to Bradley Hope being more than just a fictional character in a book or movie. I anticipate his story bringing motivation, inspiration, and renewed life to people around the world who enjoy his story.

When it looks like everything is lost and there's no way out, a little bit of hope can make all the difference.

As you go through your day today, remember all great things begin with simple hope.

Today's the day!

DARKNESS AND LIGHT

AS A BLIND PERSON, I HAVE TO CONSTANTLY REMIND MYSELF that the world is not simply divided into darkness and light. In reality, there are myriad degrees of darkness and intensities of light. I don't know if the old phrase is literally true that it is always darkest before the dawn, but I do know that in human endeavor, social change, and global progress, it is always darkest before someone turns on the light. Those who simply curse the darkness have a powerful voice until one enlightened or determined individual turns on the light. Then the naysayers, complainers, and critics simply fade into obscurity.

I have heard it said and often repeated that there has never been a monument erected to a critic. The most widely-read book among achievers and successful people is *Think and Grow Rich* by Napoleon Hill. Hill turned on the light in the midst of a vast darkness. Many of us who have written and shared our ideas since the time of Napoleon Hill have mostly reflected his light to extinguish the darkness around us.

Among Hill's many breakthrough concepts was the idea that in every adversity there is a seed of a greater good. If we extend this into our lives, every opportunity comes disguised

as a problem or challenge. The whole world is hoping and pray-
ing for a great idea, and as mentioned previously, they trip over
one about three times each week but fail to recognize it because
it appears to be a problem. All you need do to have a great idea
is to go through your daily routine, wait for something bad
to happen, and ask the powerful question, "How could I have
avoided that?" The answer to that question is a great idea. To
extend the concept a bit further, all you need to do to have a
great business is to ask one further question. "How can I help
other people avoid that problem?"

The world will give you fame, fortune, and security if you
will focus on them and help them solve their problems, but
if you choose to stand in the darkness and curse the current
conditions as opposed to simply turning on the light, you are
destined to live an unremarkable and frustrating existence.

Whenever possible in pointing out a problem to a colleague, friend, or family member, bring a potential solution to
the discussion of the problem. You can succeed in business and
in life if you become known as a problem-solver. In any organization, the person who solves the problems rises to the top.
People want to be around those individuals and follow them.
On the other hand, the person who constantly curses the darkness by pointing out every problem without offering or even
considering a solution becomes someone to avoid.

As you go through your day today, use the darkness as an
opportunity to let your light shine.

Today's the day!

OPINIONS AND OPPOSITION

WORDS HAVE WEIGHT. THEY CAN EDIFY, EDUCATE, DEPRESS, OR destroy. People reveal their biases by the words they use. If an individual clearly wants to exchange opinions with us for the purpose of learning and growing, it can be a very positive and enlightening exchange. On the other hand, if someone in the guise of asking questions has already obviously made up his or her mind, there's no reason to prolong the dialogue.

Avoid standing near people who want to open their mouths when they're not willing to open their minds.

Not long ago, I was asked to speak in Washington, DC, as a part of the National Day of Prayer ceremonies, and while there, I was also asked to make a presentation for the Wounded Warriors organization. I am always privileged and humbled to do programs for the Wounded Warriors as they bring new meaning to the word *hero*.

While in Washington, I was escorted by an Army general who was very polite and professional to my colleague and me. We were confronted several times by a reporter who convinced me he already had his mind made up and his story written. He was just looking for some background information.

He hostilely confronted me stating, "I don't see how you can call your remarks nondenominational." He went on to explain that in sharing how I was raised in my perspective, I might have offended others who were raised differently. I reminded him I had prefaced my remarks with the beautiful and powerful phrase, "In my opinion...," and I further reminded him I had shared my background, as I had clearly stated, for the purpose of helping people to understand my thoughts and perspectives. I concluded our exchange by asserting emphatically to the reporter that while I don't know everything, I am still the world's leading authority on my opinion.

As the reporter indignantly rushed away to, no doubt, file his story, the general laughed and told me he had been confronted by the same reporter just a few weeks earlier when he had asked the question, "Don't you think that, as a leader of the Army, you do nothing more than institutionalize violence?" I thought about it a moment and told the general, with all due respect, that it seemed to me institutionalized violence could be the definition of an Army. If violence isn't institutionalized, it runs rampant and touches us all, but because it's institutionalized by dedicated professionals such as my friend the general, most of us lead peaceful lives.

If someone wants to attack you or your beliefs, don't allow them to disguise it as an innocent question. Just ask them to state it clearly for the record. All legitimate questions deserve reasonable answers, but no unbridled attacks deserve any responses.

As you go through your day today, embrace others' questions and thoughts, but reject their unyielding opinions.

Today's the day!

WHAT IS IMPORTANT?

GIVING

WHETHER IT'S THE HOLIDAYS OR END-OF-YEAR TAX PLANNING, December is the time that many people think about giving. While any motivation that causes us to give is probably good, I believe we should begin to look at giving as a way to define who we are instead of simply providing a tax deduction or fulfilling our holiday gift list.

Whether it's in our personal or professional lives, we need to think about giving as an integral part of all that we do instead of an afterthought. Giving back is a way to create a true and lasting legacy. A lot of people do a good job with making money, and most everyone does a good job of spending it. But it's the giving of one's money that will yield a far more valuable return on investment. Giving does not simply apply to our money but includes our time, effort, energy, and our expertise. Any of us can give our money, and it is greatly needed and appreciated by people and causes around the world. But only you can provide the unique effort, energy, and expertise that you can bring to a particular need.

While charities need our money, the greater need is for us to begin to define ourselves as givers. The only three things you can do with your money are spend it, save/invest it, and give it away. Any brief review of headlines or recent statistics will assure you that we are doing a great job of spending our money in our society today. Unfortunately, too many people are spending all they earn and just a little more.

Far too few of us are saving and investing our money. This saving and investing is what makes the dreams we have for ourselves and our families come true. When we're spending too much and saving virtually nothing, giving becomes a random afterthought that is not a part of our daily consciousness.

Just as you should have a plan for your spending—known as a budget—and a plan for your saving/investing—known as a financial plan—you should have a conscious, specific, and well-thought-out plan for your giving. Far beyond your money, your life itself should be viewed as a gift. I believe that the meaning of life is to find our unique, special gift; and the purpose of life is to give our gift away.

People mistakenly assume that when you give something away, it's gone. In reality, if you spend your money, it disappears immediately. If you save/invest your money, it is locked away for the future. But that which we give defines us in a way so that the gift benefits others and never really leaves us.

As you go through your day today, look for new ways for your money, your work, and your life to be a gift.

Today's the day!

GREENER GRASS

MANY MISTAKES IN LIFE AND IN BUSINESS ARE MADE BECAUSE the grass seems greener in the other pasture. Invariably, as you are leaving your pasture and moving into the other pasture you thought was greener, if you are observant, you will see any number of others rushing into your pasture because it seems greener to them.

It is always a mistake to fail to take full responsibility for our current situation. One of the many tactics we all utilize is to blame our lack of success on external factors. It's very easy for us to believe that our current job, industry, location, or field of endeavor does not hold the promise that others do. This always brings us to that ongoing search for a greener pasture. Unfortunately, when you are on the outside looking in, most pastures look green because you are comparing the best attributes of the other pasture while remembering the worst aspects of your own.

The best people are succeeding in every industry. The best people are succeeding in every location. The best people are succeeding in any area of pursuit. So the question is not: Where is the greenest pasture? The question remains: Can you and I commit to becoming the best people and stay where we are?

If you find yourself involved in a pursuit that does not energize you and create passion in your heart and mind, you need to move elsewhere; but if you're just looking for an easier road to the top, you need to stay where you are.

Imagine you and I were attempting to climb a ladder to the top of a building. There are a number of ladders of various sizes, shapes, and materials in various positions all around our building. They are all different and contain unique advantages and disadvantages, but they are all safe, reliable, and lead to the top of the building.

If we pick a ladder and follow it rung by rung through advantages, disadvantages, easy times, and hard times, we will find ourselves inevitably atop the building; however, if we climb the aluminum ladder part of the way up the building while thinking how nice it would be to be climbing a wooden ladder to the point where we descend and start over—only to discover half-way up the wooden ladder that we now think the rope ladder might be best—we will do more climbing and have less to show for it than someone who picked any ladder and stuck with it to the top of the building.

As you go through your day today, look for the good things about your pasture and enjoy the green grass you already have.

Today's the day!

MULTIDIMENSIONAL

IF I WERE TO ASK YOU TO GIVE ME THE MAIN TRAIT, CHARACteristic, or ability that comes to your mind when someone mentions a race horse, you would probably think of words such as fast, speedy, or quick. If I were to ask you the same question about a grizzly bear, you might say ferocious, frightening, or deadly. While these are accurate descriptions, it might surprise you to know that a grizzly bear can outrun a race horse.

Many times, we want to do the things we do best all of the time. My late, great friend and legendary basketball coach John Wooden told me that college basketball players invariably want to dunk the ball and shoot three-point shots. Rarely do they want to practice defense or passing. Defense and passing win championships; therefore, in order to be happy and successful, we often need to become multidimensional.

If I were to ask you to visualize Tiger Woods, you would likely picture him hitting one of those towering, unbelievably long drives from the tee of a par 5 hole. Only the most avid golf fans know and appreciate the fact that, in addition to those gigantic drives, Tiger Woods has one of the highest ranked and most efficient ratings for his play out of sand traps and his putting on the green. A one-dimensional game may get you onto someone's highlight reel, but it will rarely win you championships or help you to succeed in your personal and professional life.

You may get noticed for doing one dimension of a task extremely well. You will be remembered for performing an entire job or skill at a level that makes you successful. Make a list of all of the tasks it takes for you to be successful in your current job, career, or business. Realize that each of these tasks are critical to your overall success. Don't overlook any roles within your operation.

Remember, good impressions are made or lost most often based on how your telephone is answered. If this task is done in a mediocre fashion, it will take someone on your team a tremendous amount of effort and energy to overcome that first impression. On the other hand, if your telephone is answered promptly and professionally, the stage is set for your eventual success.

Once you have a list of all the tasks required to be successful, determine which ones you will do yourself and which ones you will delegate. Delegation should not always be determined solely based upon who does the job best. A great trial lawyer might be able to answer the phone at his law firm switchboard better than anybody else; however, if the operator and receptionist can do the job 99 percent as well, the efficiencies become obvious. In order to succeed, you must have the right person at the right place at the right time doing the right thing for the right reason.

When you start out in life or in business, it may seem as though you are doing everything yourself, and, in reality, you may be; however, there will come a day when you will discover new dimensions of your own talent and have people on your team whose talents will complement and not compete with yours.

As you go through your day today, consider yourself as the coach who is assessing everyone's strengths and weaknesses so you can set the stage for your victory.

Today's the day!

COMMENCEMENT

YOU HAVE PROBABLY HEARD IT SAID—AND HAVE IT STORED somewhere in the deep recesses of your memory—that if you get a good education you'll get a good job. This message was delivered to us by well-meaning people who were right in what they said as far as it went.

We were admonished to get good grades and then we would be attractive to corporate America. Having good grades and a degree may help you get a job, but it will not help you grow, advance, or reach your goals throughout your life.

Graduation ceremonies are called commencement exercises. I believe this is because your real education commences after you leave school. Completing your formal education is not the end of learning. It is merely the beginning. Formal education is the starting line. Continuing education is the finish line that you will never fully reach.

There was a significant study done among the top executives of the largest corporations in the world to determine what characteristics or traits they had in common. Factors such as education, marital status, religious affiliation, sleep patterns, and daily exercise were explored. It was determined that the one characteristic that these leaders have in common more than any other is that they study educational, motivational, and informational material on a regular basis.

You can make a living based on what you do. You can create a life and have great success based on what you know.

While it's been said and often repeated that success is not what you know it's who you know, the fact of the matter is—success is clearly what you know, and that may lead you to who you know as you meet new people and develop new relationships.

Successful people utilize all of their time wisely. Don't forget that time driving, flying, or exercising can be turned into a post graduate course in anything you desire simply by utilizing audio books.

The Internet and search engines can be a key to focusing your continuing education in specific areas that most impact your goals and your success. The resources of the greatest libraries the world has ever known pale in comparison to what you have at your fingertips daily in the form of the Internet.

As you go through your day today, look at your formal education as the prerequisite requirement to get into the school of life as you carry out your continuing education.

Today's the day!

SAFETY NET

ALL OF US ARE STRIVING TO PAY OUR BILLS, BECOME FINAN-
cially independent, invest for the future, and save for a
comfortable retirement. These are all good things to be pursuing, but in the financial realm, just as in most areas of life, one
of the surest ways to make certain good things happen is to
keep bad things from happening. In order to protect our hard-
earned money, we need to manage the risk we can handle, and
protect ourselves against the risks we cannot handle.

Everyone's initial financial goal should be to eliminate consumer debt and establish an emergency or rainy day fund. This
emergency fund should range from six months up to one year
of your average expenditures. If you have a stable job with a
steady income that does not fluctuate, six months may be ade-
quate. If you are an entrepreneur, work in a startup venture,
or earn your income from commission, you will want to have
closer to a year's worth of expenses available at all times. This
emergency fund will allow you to take care of the inevitable
unforeseen costs that establish themselves as bumps in all of
our roads.

Your emergency fund will make sure that when your car-
buretor goes out on your car, the refrigerator dies, or your kids

require unanticipated trips to the doctor or dentist you will not go into a financial tailspin and be forced to dip into your savings and investment funds, or—even worse yet—sink into debt.

Unfortunately, life's unforeseen emergencies are not all of the small variety. For these huge, scary circumstances, we need to have insurance. Remember, no matter how confusing insurance may seem, it is nothing more or less than a group of people who share risk.

If your house burns to the ground, you probably are not ready or able to replace your home and everything in it immediately; however, if you and several hundred neighbors all put a fraction of the cost into one fund, you could collectively manage the risk if one of your houses does, indeed, burn down.

In addition to insuring your home, your possessions, and your cars, you need to insure your life. Or, to be more clear, you need to insure your ability to earn income. No one needs life insurance beyond basic burial expenses, other than people who earn an income that others are dependent upon. The exceptions to this would include nonworking spouses or partners who provide child care and household duties that would have to be otherwise handled if they unexpectedly passed away.

The most overlooked risk and the most underinsured financial area in our society today is disability insurance. If you are 32 years old, you are 12 times more likely to become disabled than you are to die before age 65. Remember, if you're disabled, not only does your income cease, but your expenses may increase due to medical needs, in-home care, etc. Ignoring risk does not make it go away.

As you go through your day today, plan to handle the risk that you can take care of yourself, and insure against the risk you can't handle on your own.

Today's the day!

THE FOLLOWING LETTER, DATED JUNE 2, 1953, IS FROM NAPOleon Hill to Barbara Braxton. Barbara is the daughter of Lee Braxton who was a friend of Napoleon Hill and mentor to Jim Stovall. Evidently, the influence of her father left a positive impact on Barbara's life. She is Dr. Barbara Braxton Wilks who retired from Oral Roberts University, where her father was one of the school's greatest supporters.

—Don Green

W. CLEMENT STONE, General Manager — RAvenswood 8-1012

NAPOLEON HILL ASSOCIATES
PUBLISHING • MOTION PICTURES
5316 SHERIDAN ROAD • CHICAGO 40, ILLINOIS.

June 2, 1953

My dear Barbara Braxton:

I have just had the privilege of reading the copies of two letters written to you by your father recently and I am taking the liberty of congratulating you on having the sort of father who could write letters like these.

Your disappointment in not having been successful in getting the job you desired is trivial in comparison with the blessings you have because of the advantages your father provided for you to become self-determining and independent.

It has been my business to know many people of all ages and I can tell you sincerely that with a father such as yours you cannot possibly fail in life unless you do not recognize the soundness of his counsel or neglect following it. You are already so very much richer—richer in every way—than the average young college graduate that you will be envied by many less fortunate young people who know you.

The letters your father sent you are so definitely classics in their field that I am asking permission of him and you to permit me to include them in a booklet I am writing to be distributed to high school students throughout the land.

I sincerely hope you will accept your father's suggestion to travel with him and thereby afford me an opportunity to meet you in person. Your father and Mr. Stone and I are engaged in a great work taking the Science of Success philosophy to an ailing world, and somehow, Barbara, I sincerely hope that in taking this success philosophy to others we shall have an opportunity to indoctrinate you and other close friends of ours with it.

Very cordially,

Napoleon Hill.

Miss Barbara Braxton
Whiteville, North Carolina.

ABOUT THE AUTHOR

JIM STOVALL is the president of Narrative Television Network, as well as a published author of many books including *The Ultimate Gift*. He is also a columnist and motivational speaker. He may be reached at 5840 South Memorial Drive, Suite 312, Tulsa, OK 74145-9082; by email at Jim@JimStovall.com; on Twitter at www.twitter.com/stovallauthor; or on Facebook at www.facebook.com/jimstovallauthor.